PROBING

THROUGH

PHILIPPIANS

by

J. VERNON MCGEE

THRU THE BIBLE BOOKS

Box 7100

PASADENA, CALIFORNIA 91109

First Printing 1972
Second Printing 1976
Third Printing 1982

Printed by
Griffin Printing & Lithograph Co., Inc.
Glendale, California 91204

CONTENTS

INTRODUCTION

The Epistle of Paul to the Philippians is one of the prison epistles. Paul wrote four epistles when he was in prison, and we have labeled them prison epistles. They are Ephesians, Philippians, Colossians, and the little epistle to Philemon.

The Epistle of Paul to the Philippians was written to the believers in Europe in the city of Philippi. This letter came out of a wonderful relationship that Paul had with the Philippian church. Actually, this church was closer to Paul than was any other church. Their love for him and his love for them is mirrored in this epistle. It deals with Christian experience at the level on which all believers should be living. It is not a level on which all of us are, but it is where God wants us to be.

Paul visited Philippi on his second missionary journey. You will recall that he and Barnabas went on their first missionary journey to the Galatian country, where they had a wonderful ministry and founded many churches in spite of the persecution they encountered. Paul wanted to visit these churches on his second missionary journey. He wanted to take Barnabas with him again, but Barnabas insisted on taking his nephew, John Mark, who had been with them at the beginning of the first missionary journey. This young fellow, John Mark, you may remember, turned chicken and ran home to Mama when they had landed on the coast of Asia Minor. And Paul did not want to take him the second time. So this split the team of Paul and Barnabas. Barnabas took John Mark and went in another direction. Paul, with Silas for a companion, retraced his steps into the Galatian country, visiting the churches which they had established on the first missionary journey.

It would seem that Paul intended to widen his circle of missionary activity in that area, because a great population was there, and it was highly civilized. Actually Greek culture and Greek learning were centered there at this particular time. Dr. Luke in recording it says that Paul attempted to go south into Asia, meaning the province of Asia, of which Ephesus was the leading city. But when he attempted to go south, the Spirit of God put up a roadblock. Since he wasn't to go south, Paul thought he would go north (where Turkey is today), but when "they assayed to go into Bithynia . . . the Spirit allowed them not" (Acts 16:7).

5

Now he can't go south, he can't go north, he has come from the east, and there isn't but one direction to go. So Paul went west as far as Troas. That was the end of the line. To go west of Troas he would have to go by boat. So Paul was waiting for instructions from God.

Sometimes we feel that God must lead us immediately, but God can let us wait. I think He lets us cool our heels many times waiting for Him to lead us. If you are one who is fretting today, "Oh, what shall I do? Which way shall I turn?" Wait, just wait. If you are really walking with the Lord, He will lead you in His own good time.

So Paul continues to wait in the city of Troas for orders, and he gets them finally. He was given the vision of the man of Macedonia.

> And a vision appeared to Paul in the night: there stood
> a man of Macedonia, beseeching him, and saying, Come
> over into Macedonia, and help us. And after he had seen
> the vision, immediately we endeavored to go into Mace-
> donia, assuredly gathering that the Lord had called us
> to preach the gospel unto them [Acts 16:9, 10].*

Paul and his companions boarded a ship that took them to the continent of Europe. To me this is the greatest crossing that ever has taken place because it took the Gospel to Europe. I am thankful for that because at this particular time my ancestors were in Europe. One family was in the forests of Germany. I am told that they were as pagan and heathen as they possibly could be. Another branch of the family was over in Scotland. And they, I am told, were the filthiest savages that ever have been on topside of this earth. Now don't you look askance at me because your ancestors were in the cave right next to my ancestors and they were just as dirty as mine were. I thank God today that the Gospel went in that direction because somewhere down the line some of these ancestors heard the Word of God, responded to it, and handed down to us a high type of civilization.

So Paul crossed over into Europe, and his first stop was Philippi.

*All Scripture quotations are from *The New Scofield Reference Bible.*

> And on the sabbath we went out of the city by a riverside, where prayer was accustomed to be made; and we sat down, and spoke unto the women who resorted there. And a certain woman, named Lydia, a seller of purple, of the city of Thyatira, who worshiped God, heard us; whose heart the Lord opened, that she attended unto the things which were spoken by Paul. And when she was baptized, and her household, she besought us, saying, If ye have judged me to be faithful to the Lord, come into my house, and abide there. And she constrained us [Acts 16:13-15].

Paul, you see, found out that the man of Macedonia was a woman by the name of Lydia, holding a prayer meeting down by the river. That prayer meeting probably had a lot to do with bringing Paul to Europe. I'm of the opinion there were many people in Philippi who saw that group of women down there by the river praying and thought it wasn't very important. But it just happened to be responsible for the greatest crossing that ever took place. And Lydia was the first convert in Europe.

Now Lydia was a member of the Philippian church to whom Paul wrote this Epistle. We know something about some of the other members of this church also. There was a girl who was delivered from demon possession.

> And it came to pass, as we went to prayer, a certain maid possessed with a spirit of divination met us, who brought her masters much gain by soothsaying. The same followed Paul and us, and cried, saying, These men are the servants of the Most High God, who show unto us the way of salvation. And this did she many days. But Paul, being grieved, turned and said to the spirit, I command thee, in the name of Jesus Christ, to come out of her. And he came out the same hour [Acts 16:16-18].

Also the Philippian jailer and his family were members of this church. You recall that Paul and Silas were thrown into jail at the instigation of the masters of the demon possessed girl who had been deprived of their income. God intervened for Paul and Silas in such a miraculous way that their jailer came to know Christ.

> And [the jailer] brought them out, and said, Sirs, what must I do to be saved? And they said, Believe on the Lord Jesus Christ, and thou shalt be saved, and thy house. . . . And when he had brought them into his house, he set food before them, and rejoiced, believing in God with all his house [Acts 16:30, 31, 34].

There were, of course, other members of this Philippian church whose stories we do not know. They were a people very close to the Apostle Paul. They followed him in his journeys and ministered to him time and time again. But when Paul was arrested in Jerusalem, they lost sight of him for two years. They did not know where he was. Finally they heard that he was in Rome in prison. The hearts of these people went out to him, and immediately they dispatched their pastor, Epaphroditus, with a gift that would minister to Paul's needs.

So Paul wrote this epistle to thank the church and to express his love for them. He had no doctrine to correct as he did in his epistle to the Galatians. Neither did he have to correct their conduct, as he did in his epistle to the Corinthians. There was only one small ripple in the fellowship of the church between two women, Euodia and Syntyche, and Paul gives them a word of admonishment near the end of his letter. He didn't seem to treat it as being serious.

His letter to the Philippian believers is the great epistle of Christian experience. That is his subject in Paul's Epistle to the Philippians.

There are four chapters in this Epistle, and they divide like this:

Chapter 1—*Philosophy* of Christian Living
Chapter 2—*Pattern* for Christian Living
Chapter 3—*Prize* for Christian Living
Chapter 4—*Power* for Christian Living

Although this is a very simple outline, I feel it is quite adequate, and I will follow it as I attempt to deal with this Epistle in depth.

PHILOSOPHY
OF CHRISTIAN LIVING

Outline:

1. *Introduction, verses 1, 2*
2. *Paul's Tender Feeling for the Philippians, verses 3-11*
3. *Bonds and Afflictions Further the Gospel, verses 12-20*
4. *In Life or Death—Christ, verses 21-30*

INTRODUCTION *verses 1, 2*

1   **Paul and Timothy, the servants of Jesus Christ, to all the saints in Christ Jesus who are at Philippi, with the bishops and deacons.**

The opening verse is very rich. Notice how Paul associates Timothy with himself—**Paul and Timothy.** Paul is constantly identifying with himself certain young preachers. In his ministry he will bring Titus with him; he will bring Silas with him. I think it is a very lovely way of doing because these young men were starting out in the ministry.

Within the space of just a few weeks I have been in about twenty churches and have met many pastors. I have discovered that the most discouraged men in this country are pastors. Because I was a pastor for forty years, I can empathize with them. They are having a rough time today. In Detroit the other day the pastor of one of the leading churches walked out of the pulpit and said, "I'm through." Now he is selling automobiles. He said, "I'd rather do that than fool with the church." I talked to a young preacher in Ohio. I sat with him in a restaurant the other night as he poured out his heart to me about the problem he is having. It is a privilege to encourage these young pastors whom I meet. They are in Bible churches; they are in small churches. Many of them are doing a great work. They *need* encouragement in this hour in which we are living, friend. The pastor is supposed to be ministering to other people, but he needs ministering to also. I love Paul's interest in young preachers— "Paul and Timothy." He brings Timothy right by his side.

The servants of Jesus Christ. Notice that Paul calls himself a servant of Jesus Christ. Contrast this to his epistle to the Galatians where he was defending his apostleship. Paul is breathing fire when he opens that epistle. He begins it, "Paul, an apostle"—he wants them to know that. "Paul, an apostle (not of men, neither by man)." In other words Paul is declaring, "I'm an apostle, not because I went to school to become an apostle, not because men placed their hands on my head and I went through a ceremony. I'm an apostle of Jesus Christ—He himself made me an apostle!" Well, Paul didn't write that in this Epistle to the Philippians. The folk at Philippi loved him. He did not have to defend his apostleship. And he takes his rightful position with Timothy, both servants of Jesus Christ. Literally the word is *bondslave*—"Paul and Timothy, bondslaves of Jesus Christ."

Now notice to whom his letter is addressed: **To all the saints.** This means it is to all the believers. The saints are not just a peculiar group of believers. They are *all* the believers. There are only two groups of people in the world: the saints and the ain'ts. If you are saved, you're a saint—not because of your conduct, but because of your position in Christ. That is the thing that is important.

He makes this clear by the next phrase, **In Christ Jesus who are at Philippi.** Notice they are *in* Christ Jesus, and they are *at* Philippi. In . . . at. They could have been "at" anyplace. Though it's not good grammar, let me say it is not where you're *at*, but it's who you're *in* that is important. *In* Christ. Personally I consider this little word *in* to be one of the most important words in the New Testament. For me it just leaped from the page quite a few years ago. The preposition *in* when it precedes *Christ*, or a pronoun that refers to Him, is the most important word that we have in the New Testament. What does it mean to be saved? I asked a theology professor this question not long ago while I was having lunch with him. "What is your theological terminology for being saved?" Believe me, he gave me quite a lecture, and I was a little dizzy when he finished. He elucidated on the word *propitiation.* That's a good word, and it's a Bible word. Also he defined *reconciliation* and *redemption.* Now all of these are marvelous words, and they are Bible words, but not one of them covers the entire spectrum of salvation.

The Spirit of God chose just one little word, the preposition *in,* to explain what salvation is. What does it mean to be saved? It means to be *in* Christ. How do you get in Christ? Well, you get in Christ when you trust Him as your Savior, when you accept Him as your Savior.

> For by one Spirit were we all baptized into one body, whether we be Jews or Greeks, whether we be bond or free . . . [1 Corinthians 12:13].

How do you get in Christ? By the baptism of the Holy Spirit. When does that take place? The moment you trust Christ as Savior. When you are saved, you are put in the body of believers. The Holy Spirit identifies you with Christ, puts you *in* Christ. The saints in Philippi were saved. They had gotten in Christ. They were in the body of believers. They were there by the baptism of the Holy Spirit.

Notice now Paul's formal introduction:

2   Grace be unto you, and peace, from God, our Father, and from the Lord Jesus Christ.

You find this in all Paul's epistles, and you find *grace* and *peace* in that sequence. He never turns it around. It is **grace to you and peace** Let's take a moment to look at these words because of their importance.

Grace was the word of greeting in the Greek world, and in the Greek language it is *charis.* Had you been walking down the street in any port or any city of the Roman Empire, you would have heard folk greeting each other with the word *Charis,* Grace. It was the Gentile form of greeting. I walked down the streets of Athens with Nick Simponis, a Greek missionary. As we walked along, Nick would way something that sounded to me like "Charis" when he would meet somebody, and they would respond with the same word. So I asked him, "Did I understand you to say, "Charis?" He laughed and said, "Well, I didn't pronounce it like that, but that's what I meant." You see, modern Greek has come through several stages, and though they are the same words, they are not pronounced the same. I asked him, "Is that still a greeting?" "Yes," he said, "that's a greeting for us." Grace, *charis,* was a secular form of greeting.

Peace is the religious form of greeting. You would have to go to Jerusalem to hear that. If you had walked down a Jerusalem street and met a fellow with a long beard and a hat, he would have said, "Shalom, shalom," meaning "peace."

Now Paul took these two words, *grace* and *peace,* and brought them up to the highest level. You and I are saved by the grace of God. Theologians call *grace* "unmerited favor." That's all right, but I'm just a poor preacher, so I call it "love in action." That's what grace is: love in action. Let me put it like this: God does not save us by love. I hear people say that God saved them by His love. No, my friend, God didn't save you by love. What's the verse?

> For by grace are ye saved through faith; and that
> not of yourselves, it is the gift of God—not of works, lest
> any man should boast [Ephesians 2:8, 9].

Isn't there a verse about God's love? Yes.

> For God so loved the world, that he gave his only
> begotten Son, that whosoever believeth in him should not
> perish, but have everlasting life [John 3:16].

God so loved the world that He saved the world? No. It is true that God loves every sinner. I find it very difficult to love some folk, but God loves them. And Jesus died for them. God loved Hitler, and Jesus died for him. But that doesn't mean he was saved. You see, God doesn't save by love. He saves by grace. God is more than love. God is holy; God is righteous; God is just. God can't open the back door of heaven and bring sinners in under cover of darkness. God is holy and righteous, and He can no more do that than a judge can let a criminal off when a bribe is slipped to him under the counter. My friend, He has to be just; He has to be righteous. God cannot arbitrarily, like a sob-sister, just reach down and bring sinners into heaven. Love provided a Savior. God so loved that He gave His only begotten Son to make a way for sinners to come on a righteous, holy ground so that He could save them. God can hold out His arms to a lost world and say, "I love you, but I can only save you by grace. You haven't anything to give Me. I have everything to give you now that Christ has paid the penalty for your sins."

The idea is abroad today that we can somehow bring God down to our level. I met a hippie on the streets of the French quarter down in New Orleans who had been given the viewpoint that Jesus was some sort of a buddy, down on his level. Now let me get this off my chest and I'll feel better if I do. I do not like these little sweet songs that say "Jesus is a friend of mine." We need to be very careful when we say things like that or sing things like that. Listen to Him:

Ye are my friends, if ye do whatever I command you [John 15:14].

Now don't sing a song like that unless you are obeying Him. Don't think that you can bring Him down to your level.

Let me illustrate this. Suppose that I would say that the President of the United States is a friend of mine. I would bring him down to the level of Vernon McGee. But suppose the President would say, "Vernon McGee is a friend of mine." He would bring me up to his level. Don't try to bring Jesus down to your level by running around and saying, "Jesus is a friend of mine." The question is: Are you obeying Him? He says, "You are my friend if you do what I command you." You are His friend, not just because you are saved, but because you do what He commands you. And that brings us up to His level. Oh, this business today of trying to bring Him down to the level of little man! God, my friend, saves us by His marvelous, infinite, wonderful grace. It is wonderful that God saved Vernon McGee. How gracious of Him to do that!

When you know you have been saved by the grace of God, then you can have the peace of God, the peace of God in your heart. Peace is something, I'm convinced, that is needed today by multitudes of folk. All of us carry around a guilt complex. We can't get rid of it. A professor out at the University of Southern California, quite a few years ago, attended our Bible study, and heard me mention the guilt complex one night. Afterward he said to me, "McGee, you don't emphasize that enough. Your guilt complex is as much a part of you as your right arm. We psychologists know how to shift it from one place to another, and when we do we make an odd-ball out of the person. We can shift it, but we can't remove it. The only place I know of that you can get rid of a guilt complex is at the cross of Christ." That's where you can get rid of it, friend. All of us stand guilty before Almighty God. He is our Judge. And the only One who can lay any charge against God's elect is God who justifies. After we are in Christ, the only One who can bring a charge against us says, "You are not guilty, because My Son died for you and you have accepted Him." You see, there are only two places for sin. Either your sin—right now—is on you, or it is on Christ. If it is on you, you are yet to come for judgment. Believe me, you are to be judged one of these days, and you have that guilt complex whether you will acknowledge it or not. But, my friend, if you have accepted Christ, your guilt is on Him, and the judgment is passed. You have passed from death to life—nothing but life before you. And today the One who is the Judge is not condemning you. He is your Savior, and the throne of God is a throne of *grace* to which sinners can come. And when they come they can have the peace of God in their hearts. Where are your sins right now? Let's get right down to the nitty-gritty. Have you accepted Christ as your Savior and are your sins on Christ? If they are, you will have peace in your heart because He bore your sins. "Therefore, being justified by faith, we have peace with God through our Lord Jesus Christ" (Romans 5:1). If your sin is still on you, you won't sleep too well because you are going to come to judgment some day. But God wants to give you His peace. It can be yours because of what Christ has done for you.

PAUL'S TENDER FEELING
FOR THE PHILIPPIANS, *verses 3-11*

Paul completes his introduction in the first two verses, then in the third verse he begins the body of his letter in a very lovely manner. This section reveals the sweet relationship between Paul and the Philippian believers. And this is the way it ought to be today among believers, especially between pastor and congregation. This is something that I'm afraid is being greatly neglected, and it gives a wrong testimony to the world outside. Now listen to Paul:

3   **I thank my God upon every remembrance of you.**

Can you think of a lovelier thing to say to someone than that? Now I have learned over the years that when I get a letter from a brother that begins with, "I thank my God upon every remembrance of you," he is going to ask me for something. My immediate reaction is, "I wonder what he wants." And as I read the letter I soon find out. He is after something. I'm not sure he thanks God upon every remembrance of me, and if I don't grant his request, I *know* he won't be thanking God upon every remembrance of me. However, it is a lovely thing to hear when it is genuine, when it is real and original. Paul says to the Philippian believers that with every remembrance of them he thanks God.

Imagine a church like that! I was walking with a preacher friend of mine along a street in downtown Los Angeles quite a few years ago, when he suddenly grabbed my arm and pulled me aside, saying, "Look in this window."

I said, "What in the world is there here to look at?"

"Nothing," he said, "but that couple coming down the street, we don't want to meet them." So we put our heads down there right by the window, and in a few moments they passed by.

"Are they that bad?"

"Oh, they're that bad! You don't want to meet them."

"Well, then this is a couple to whom you couldn't say, 'I thank God upon every remembrance of you.' "

"No," he said, "you sure couldn't."

My, it is wonderful to be a church, or a family, or a couple or an individual of whom it can be said, "I thank God upon every remembrance of you."

4   **Always in every prayer of mine for you all making request with joy.**

Notice the word **always**—not just sometimes. *Always* in *every* prayer Paul remembered the Philippian believers. When I was teaching the Epistles in the classroom years ago, I would have the students list the prayers of Paul. When we would be studying the Epistle to the Philippians they would have to put down on Paul's prayer list the Philippian believers. After we had been through Paul's epistles student after student came to me and said, "I never realized how many people Paul prayed for." He had quite a prayer list. By the way, how long is *your* prayer list? For how many people do you pray? It is wonderful to have a long prayer list. Paul had one.

Notice also that he said to the Philippians, "Always in every prayer of mine for **you all** . . ." When we reach the last chapter of this Epistle we will find there was one little ripple of discord in the Philippian church. Two women, Syntyche and Euodia, were not speaking to each other. So Paul was very careful at the very beginning to include all the saints in order that one group couldn't say to the other, "He is writing to us and not to you."

Many men who write on the Epistle to the Philippians call it the "Joy Epistle." I have never called it that although I recognize that the word *joy* occurs 19 times and is an important word. There is a great emphasis upon joy because if we are living the Christian life we are going to have joy in our hearts. Joy, I think, is the barometer of your Christian life. Are you having joy? Living for Christ should not be an ordeal; it should be fun! Christ wants there to be joy in your life.

You can call this the "Joy" Epistle if you want to, but if you are going to call it that just because *joy* occurs 19 times, then I suggest you call it the "Christ" Epistle because that occurs over 40 times. And I believe that the very center and heart of this Epistle is the Person of Jesus Christ. As we shall see, the philosophy of Christian living has to do with Him; the pattern has to do with Him; the prize has to do with Him; the power has to do with Him. Actually it is a personal relationship with Christ that brings joy to a believer's life.

Now having told them he thanked God for them, he gives a reason:

5   **For your fellowship in the gospel from the first day until now.**

You can see that the Philippians from the time Paul came to them as a missionary in the beginning were close to him. They had fellowship with him in the Gospel.

Let's not pass over this word **fellowship.** I know of no word that's been so abused as the word *fellowship.* The world outside uses it a great deal today. For quite a few years I was invited to speak to a Rotary Club. The chairman of their program committee was a doctor, and he used to call me and say, "I think they can take you about once a year, so you come and give them both barrels because you won't be here again for a year." So I'd be there for either the Christmas program or the Easter program. Above the speaker's table they had the slogan "Food, Fun, Fellowship." I looked at that and thought, *Oh, boy. The Rotary Club is stealing from the church.* Those three things belong to the church. The early church had all three. But, frankly, I didn't see why they put that sign up there because the food was embalmed chicken with peas as big as cannon balls, and the fun was corny jokes, and the fellowship, as best I could tell, was patting somebody on the back and saying, "Hello, Bill. How's business?" Well, friends, that's not fellowship in the Bible sense. The word in the Greek is *koinōnia* which means "communion"; it means that which believers can share of the things of Christ. For instance, a Bible study is a fellowship when we are sharing the things of Christ. Paul used the word *fellowship* when speaking of the Lord's Supper, when reading the Scriptures, when praying, when taking up an offering. Anything that believers could share together was a *koinōnia,* the sharing of the things of Christ.

Let me illustrate. Over in England at Oxford University there is a college that teaches nothing but Shakespeare. Suppose you went over there, and at the first session you sat down at the board for the evening meal and heard the professors and first and second year students talking back and forth about Shakespeare. Maybe you'd hear someone quote one of Romeo's lines: "The all seeing sun has never seen her likes since first the world begun." And you would hear them say that Romeo didn't say that about Juliet, but about another girl! And you had thought Romeo was the most constant lover! So you start going to classes, and pulling books off the shelves, and before long you get acquainted with Shakespeare. After you've been there at the college for two years, they call you in, put a hood on you, put a certificate in your hand, and make you a fellow. Now you go in and sit down at the board. And when the professors and the other students talk about Shakespeare, *you* begin to talk about Shakespeare. You know what they know, and you begin to share the things of Shakespeare. You are a fellow; you are having fellowship.

Fellowship is a word we need to recover for the church, for believers. And it doesn't necessarily mean a church dinner, because often there is no fellowship there at all. They have a toastmaster who tells corny jokes, and there is some sort of entertainment, but no fellowship. Fellowship is when we share the things of Christ. This is what Paul is talking about. "For your fellowship in the gospel from the first day until now." They shared with Paul in their giving that the Gospel of Jesus Christ might go out. That was fellowship. And you have fellowship when you give anything that is getting out the Word of God.

The next verse is my life verse, and it is very meaningful to me:

6   Being confident of this very thing, that he who hath begun a good work in you will perform it until the day of Jesus Christ.

The day of Jesus Christ is the time He takes His own out of the world, which He has been doing for the past 1900 years.

He who hath begun a good work in you will perform it right down to the very end. In other words, "He is able also to save them to the uttermost that come unto God by him" (Hebrews 7:25).

Because this verse means a great deal to me, I hope you won't mind my being personal. Back in the days when I went to college there was no subsidizing or scholarships, and I had to work my way through. Every year I thought I would not be able to go back to college the following year, but somehow God would open up a job and I'd be able to continue in school. On graduation day, after receiving my degree, I returned to my room in the dormitory, still in my cap and gown, and sat dejectedly on the edge of my bed. My roommate came and asked, "What in the world—did somebody die?" I said, "Just as well to. I thought God called me to the ministry. I'm through college, the depression has hit and I do not even have a job this summer. I haven't a dime to go to seminary next year." While we were still talking, the phone rang. It was for me. On the other end of the line was a dear little lady who asked me to stop by her home where she lived with her sister. They were both widows, and they looked as if they had come out of the ante-bellum days. They attended the church where I taught a class of intermediate boys, and herded them into the church service every Sunday morning. They sat in the pew behind us and I always thought they disapproved. But in their home that day each handed me an envelope in memory of her husband. I left as soon as it was polite to go, hurried around the corner and opened the envelopes. The first contained a check for $250.00; I hurriedly opened the other envelope and found another check for $250.00. Do you know what $500.00 was like during the Depression? I felt like a millionaire! I was never so thrilled in my life. So that night there was given to me this verse: "Being confident of this very thing, that he who hath begun a good work in you will perform it until the day of Jesus Christ." And may I say to you that from that day until this, that verse has been true.

Now let me ask you a question. If you are a child of God I am sure you can give a similar testimony. Can't you look back over your life and see how He's led you and provided for you? Well, then, why are you worried today? Why are you concerned about tomorrow? Do you think He is going to let you down now? Many of us Christians act like unbelievers. In fact, we act like practical atheists! Oh, you've had your problems, you've had your sorrows, you've had some dark nights, but He has never let you down. This is a wonderful verse. I've taken it with me to the hospital, and I found it worked in the hospital. I've taken this verse with me to many places. You can take it with you anywhere, friend. Just lay it out before the Lord and tell Him, "Well, I'm trusting You. I'm resting in You."

7   **Even as it is right for me to think this of you all, because I have you in my heart, inasmuch as both in my bonds, and in the defense and confirmation of the gospel, ye all are partakers of my grace.**

I have you in my heart—isn't that a wonderful place to carry folk? Sometimes we reach for our billfold and say, "I want to show you a picture." Paul says, "I have the picture of the Philippians with me. It's not in my billfold, it's in my heart. I carry them in my heart."

Partakers of my grace brings us back to the word *fellowship*. It is *koinōnia* with a preposition that intensifies it: *sugkoinōnous*, meaning "a sharing together." As it was said of David, "bound in the bundle of life with the Lord thy God." What a picture this is!

8   **For God is my witness, how greatly I long after you all in the tender mercies of Jesus Christ.**

If you are reading from the Authorized Version of the Bible, you will see that **tender mercies** is "bowels"; these new translations have toned it down because it seems a bit crude. One night at Bible Study I was teaching this, and I toned it down. One of the psychologists at the University of Southern California, who regularly attended the Bible Study, got after me for it. He said, "The ancients were right. They were accurate when they talked about our feelings being in the region of the bowels." He tapped me on the forehead and said, "Very little takes place up here" (I felt that he really knew *me* when he said that), "but in the abdominal region we live and move and have our being." Paul is saying, "I long after you in the tenderest way possible." It would be difficult to put that feeling into words. Have you ever been away from home and had that homesickness for some loved one? How do you describe it? That is what Paul is talking about. Look where he is. He is in Rome, in prison, and mad Nero is on the throne. And here this church in Philippi has sent him a gift and a wonderful message expressing their love to him. Oh, the feeling he had for those believers! "I long after you with the tenderest feelings imaginable." What a wonderful relationship it was. How we need to have genuine love and concern for each other in Christian circles today!

9
10   **And this I pray, that your love may abound yet more and more in knowledge and in all judgment; that ye may approve things that are excellent; that ye may be**
11   **sincere and without offense till the day of Christ, being filled with the fruits of righteousness, which are by Jesus Christ, unto the glory and praise of God.**

I pray—here is another thing he prayed for. Paul prayed that their **love** might abound, and that it might abound in **judgment** and **knowledge**. This is something we need today, and I think we need it desperately. We are going through a phase of lovey-dovey stuff. We hear so much talk about loving everybody. For instance, the theme song of the hippie world is love and peace. A young man up in San Mateo began to talk to me about peace. He said, "Dr. McGee, why don't you talk about peace? Why don't you talk against war?"

I said, "Wait just a minute. There is something far more important than that. First we need peace in the human heart, a peace with God through the forgiveness of sins." I finally asked him the question, "Really, is it peace in the world that you want or peace in your heart?"

"It's peace in my heart that I really want," he admitted.

I am convinced that when you hear all this clamor about world peace, the average youngster needs peace in his heart. Today we hear a lot of talk about peace and loving everybody. Now let's not beat around the bush about this. Do we love everybody? Are we called upon to love everybody? When Paul says, "Let your love abound more and more," he is not saying to let it slop over on every side, but to let it abound "in knowledge and in all judgment." What does he mean? Let me illustrate from my own experience.

When I first went to downtown Los Angeles as pastor of the Church of the Open Door, I soon found that there are certain groups that move through that downtown area and prey on church people and new preachers especially. One Sunday morning one of the personal workers came to me and said, "There's a man here who has come forward and wants to talk to you about his salvation." Well, I felt complimented. The man wants to talk to *me;* he won't talk to anybody else. So I went over to talk to him, and by that time practically everybody had left the church. I began to explain the plan of salvation. I never saw a fellow so interested. He would take my Bible and read the verses I indicated. Oh, he had it down to a system! Finally I asked him if he wanted to accept Christ. Tears came to his eyes and ran down his face. He said yes, he did. We got down on our knees, and he prayed. When we stood up, I made a mistake. I asked him how he was getting along. And he told me, "I hate to tell you this, but my suitcase is down here in a certain hotel. They won't let me have it because I owe them $7.00." Well, what would you do? You had just led a man to the Lord, supposedly; you're a Christian; you're a preacher; you ought to love the brother. Well, I gave him the $7.00, and I felt expansive. I told my wife about it, and felt very good inside that I had been so generous. About six weeks after that I was going through the daily paper, and there was a picture of this man. I thought, *How in the world did he get into the paper?* And I read that he'd been arrested. He had spent the past six months in Los Angeles living off the preachers, and his comment was, "They are the biggest saps in the world." And I was one of them! I called up Dr. Bob Schuler who was still in downtown Los Angeles at Trinity Methodist Church, and asked, "Did this fellow come down to you?" "Yes," he said. "Did you let him have $7.00?" He said, "No. That's what he wanted, but I've been down here a long time, Vernon. After you've been down here awhile, you'll find there are some you can't love."

Paul says to let your love abound more and more, but let it abound in judgment, let it abound in being able to discern. Over the years when I would drive to my study in Los Angeles I used to say to the Lord, "I'm going to meet new people today, and I don't know them. Some of them I'll be able to help. Others of them will put a knife in my back. Lord, help me to be able to distinguish between the two. Show me which I should help." Actually this verse rescues a Christian from being naive and gullible. His love is to abound in knowledge and discernment.

BONDS AND AFFLICTIONS
FURTHER THE GOSPEL, *verses 12-20*

12   But I would ye should understand, brethren, that the things which happened unto me have fallen out rather unto the furtherance of the gospel.

We can understand why Paul is saying this to the Philippian believers. They had sent a message to him by their pastor, Epaphroditus, and it probably went something like this: "Oh, Brother Paul, our hearts go out to you. How terrible it was that the religious rulers in Jerusalem seized you and you're in prison in Rome. And the Gospel is being hindered because of that." Now a lot of saints are well-meaning in this type of sympathy, but notice with what wonderful optimism Paul answers them: **The things which happened unto me have fallen out rather unto the furtherance of the gospel.** In other words, "Instead of my imprisonment being a hindrance, it has actually furthered the Gospel."

Do you know that the richest years of the church were the first 200 years? Believers almost evangelized the world! They evangelized the Roman Empire—then they bogged down. Augustine wrote *The City of God,* then the church started building a kingdom down here on this earth. It doesn't have much to show for it today, but that's what it has been doing. It lost sight of its great purpose to evangelize the world. What Paul is saying is that persecution does not hinder the Gospel. The fastest growth of the church was during the period of the martyrs. There have been several periods of persecution, and in each case the church has emerged greatly strengthened. Persecution has never hurt the church. The thing that hurts the church is prosperity. In America today it is our affluent society that is hurting the church. Persecution and imprisonment for Paul furthered the Gospel.

Someone says, "Now, Brother Paul, it is very easy to make a bold statement like that, but what do you mean?" So Paul gets down to the nitty-gritty and gives two specifics that reveal the Gospel had been furthered by his arrest and incarceration.

13   **So that my bonds in Christ are manifest in all the palace, and in all other places.**

Palace should be properly translated "Caesar's court." When we come to the conclusion of this Epistle, Paul says, "All the saints greet you, chiefly they that are of Caesar's household" (Philippians 4:22). In other words, there were saints in Caesar's household, in the family of Caesar. We think of the Caesars being a very brutal, cruel, pagan lot, and they were, but also there were those in the royal family who had come to a knowledge of Christ.

How could such a thing take place? Well, when God waylaid Paul on the Damascus Road, and sent Ananias to him, He said there were two things about this man that would be unusual. One was: "I will show him how great things he must suffer for my name's sake" (Acts 9:16). I believe Paul suffered more than any other believer has suffered. And I think the reason God permitted that was so no saint could complain, "Oh, I'm suffering more than anyone!" No, my friend, you haven't suffered as much as Paul suffered. Regardless of the intensity of your suffering, you can be sure that since God brought Paul through it, He will bring you through it also.

Another thing God said of Paul was that he was "a chosen vessel unto me, to bear my name before the Gentiles, and kings, and the children of Israel" (Acts 9:15). Now up to the time of Paul's arrest, he had never, as far as I can learn, appeared before rulers or kings. But the minute they arrest him, here he goes before Roman rulers—before governors Felix and Festus, before King Agrippa, then they put him in chains and send him to Rome, since he had appealed to Caesar. In Rome he was not first put in the Mamertine prison, but in a hired house, under the charge of the Praetorian Guard, who were members of the royal family. So that every four hours, at the change of the guard, one soldier after another would come and chain himself to the Apostle Paul. These soldiers were the elite of Roman patricians, and were members of Caesar's household. What do you think Paul talked about during those four hours? Imagine having your congregation chained to you! They couldn't even walk out on you. I can imagine that some of them were happy to see their relief guard come, and would say, "Boy, am I glad to see you! This man Paul is trying to make a Christian out of me." And some of them came to know Christ. The Gospel penetrated Caesar's household. Later Tertullian wrote that the Roman government became disturbed about it when it was discovered that Christians were in positions of authority. They were so loyal to Christ that they would not even take a pinch of incense and sprinkle it before an image of Caesar, which, in the eyes of Rome, made them traitors to their country. They would rather die than have Jesus Christ brought down to the level of any of the gods of the Roman Empire. The Roman government sent spies to a meeting place of the Christians, and brought back a report that went something like this: These Christians are strange people. They meet in a very plain room that has no image, no idol, no picture. They talk about One by the name of Jesus who is absent. They seem to be expecting Him at any moment. And how they love Him and each other!

By the way, suppose Russia had sent over some spies to find out if there is anything to Christianity. And suppose a spy came into your church and then went back to report. What do you think he would have to tell? Would he be able to say, "My, how those Christians love each other, and how they love Jesus Christ and look for Him"? We have come a long ways in 1900 years, haven't we?

Paul, you see, was able to reach into Caesar's household with the Gospel, and so he says, "The things which happened unto me have fallen out rather unto the furtherance of the gospel."

Not only did Paul's imprisonment enable him to reach into Caesar's household with the Gospel, but it accomplished something else:

14   **And many of the brethren in the Lord, becoming confident by my bonds, are much more bold to speak the word without fear.**

Do you see the situation? Although Paul's appearance was probably unattractive, he must have been a tremendous speaker. After hearing him a Christian would say, "Man, I'd like to witness for the Lord, but I can't tell it like he tells it." And as long as Paul was out preaching the Gospel, a great many folk said, "I can't do it like that so I'll keep quiet." But one day word went down Roman roads to all these centers where churches had been established that Paul the apostle was in prison in Rome. Do you know what happened? In many of these churches men said, "Look, he's in prison and he can't go out any more. So I'll go." And many men started out to preach the Gospel.

And I know their feeling. Years ago when Dr. Harry Ironside became ill, Dr. Chafer called me from Dallas Theological Seminary and said, "Vernon, would you come over and take Dr. Ironside's lectures here? He's sick." Well, I went over there, but I was frightened. I was to stand before about 250 fellows who had sat under the teaching of Dr. Ironside. I could imagine them saying, "Imagine *him* trying to take Dr. Ironside's place. What a comparison!" I'll be honest with you, I went there on my knees. I was frightened. But during that year Dr. Ironside died, and Dr. Chafer called me in and said, "Dr. Ironside, as you know, has gone home to be with the Lord. Now we want to ask you to take his lectures." Do you know that I went there the next year without fear? Do you know why? I looked at those fellows and thought, *You may think you want to hear Dr. Ironside, but he's not coming any more, boys. You've got me now, and you're going to have to listen to me.* I went there with confidence. I know the feeling of many Christians in the Roman Empire in that day when they heard that the Apostle Paul was imprisoned. I think literally hundreds of witnesses went out. Paul sat back in prison and said, "Say, this is great. I never could get those fellows to move before, and now they are out as missionaries for Christ. The things which happened to me have happened for the furtherance of the Gospel."

Now Paul's imprisonment had another benefit that he does not mention. He may not have realized the importance of his writing, but if he had not been put in prison, we would not have the Prison Epistles. We would not be able to study the Epistle to the Philippians; there would have been no such letter. Paul was accurate when he said, "The things which happened have been for the furtherance of the Gospel."

There was, however, a difficulty, and Paul now mentions this:

15   **Some, indeed, preach Christ even of envy and strife; and some also of good will.**

He is going to have a great deal to say about envy and strife in the second chapter. In passing, let me way that I haven't seen a church yet that does not have problems. And I think you can resolve all of them around these two words: envy and strife. Those are the two.

16   **The one preach Christ of contention, not sincerely, supposing to add affliction to my bonds.**

There were those who were envious of the Apostle Paul. They had not been able to say anything against him, but now he's in prison, unable to defend himself. So when these men go out, they preach the Gospel, they preach Christ, but they also have a few little things to say about Paul. For instance, they said, "You folk thought Paul was a great apostle. Do you know that he was not one of the original Twelve? He wasn't near as great as you folk thought he was." And that word was coming back to the Apostle Paul, who says:

17   **But the other, of love, knowing that I am set for the defense of the gospel.**

This verse, by the way, ought to give us a different attitude toward many preachers today who may not be doing it the way we think they ought to do it. We need to be very careful about criticizing any man who preaches the Gospel. I recognize that there is no one who has been as hard on the Pentecostals as I've been. But I have found there are some wonderful people among them. A Pentecostal preacher has invited me to hold meetings in his church, and I asked him the question, "Why in the world, after all the mean things I say about you folk, would you invite me?" This man, with tears in his eyes, said, "Brother McGee, you stand for the Word of God and the Gospel that we preach." And I said, "Brother, I'd like to jump all over you, but can't jump all over you when you talk like that!" Many folk disagree with us, yet they stand for the inerrancy of Scripture; they hold to the deity of Christ; and they preach the substitutionary, vicarious, redemptive death of Christ. We need to be very careful about criticizing other believers because we are becoming a small crowd today. You talk about a minority group—believers are a minority group in this world today, and we do well not to try to kill each other.

Look at Paul's reaction to these folk who were criticizing him, those who "preach Christ of contention, not sincerely, supposing to add affliction to my bonds." Will he hit back at them?

18 **What then? Notwithstanding, every way, whether in pretense or in truth, Christ is preached; and in that I do rejoice, yea, and will rejoice.**

Regardless of their attack on him, he rejoices that they are preaching the Gospel.

The other evening I drove down "church row" in a certain city. I found that all the great churches were closed up Sunday night. But one church was just jumping—people all over the place. And I said, "Well, I know one thing: that man in there is preaching the Word of God." I disagree with him very severely on several things, but he's preaching Christ, and I'll rejoice. Sometimes I feel like bowing my head in shame when I hear the *way* Christ is being preached, but I rejoice that He is being preached. We need to be very careful about our criticism. Paul said, "Christ is preached; and in that I do rejoice, yea, and will rejoice."

19 **For I know that this shall turn to my salvation through your prayer, and the supply of the Spirit of Jesus Christ.**

By the word **salvation** Paul means his deliverance from prison that he might come to the church at Philippi.

20 **According to my earnest expectation and my hope, that in nothing I shall be ashamed, but that with all boldness, as always, so now also Christ shall be magnified in my body, whether it be by life or by death.**

Chapter 1, you recall, gives the philosophy of Christian living. You will find that Paul will sum up the theme of each of these four chapters in one verse—and sometimes in one sentence. The next verse puts Chapter 1 in a nutshell. It is only one sentence (and the verb is not there—notice it is printed in italics in your Bible):

IN LIFE OR DEATH—CHRIST, *verses 21-30*

21 **For to me to live Christ, and to die gain.**

This is the philosophy of Christian living—"to live Christ, and to die gain." Dr. Pettingill used to say that **gain** is always more of the same thing. And if to live is Christ, then to die would be more of Christ. And it means to go and to be with Him.

Now we know why Paul was undisturbed by the criticism being leveled at him. You can't hurt a man like this. It reminds me of old Chrysostom, one of the early church fathers of the first century. The emperor wanted to frighten the daylights out of him, and threatened, "I'll take away from you your property."

Chrysostom replied, "You cannot take away my property or my treasure. It is in heaven."

"Then I'll take away your loved ones."

"Oh, my loved ones have already gone to heaven."

"Then I'll put you in solitary confinement."

"You cannot put me in solitary confinement for Jesus has promised to go with me and to never forsake me."

"Then I shall put you to death."

"If you do that, I'll thank you because you will transport me right into His presence."

The emperor went back and called a huddle. What could they do to such a man! "For me to live Christ, and to die gain" is a high plane on which to live. I wish I could say I'm up there. I'm on my way, but I haven't arrived.

Paul did not know what his future would be.

22
23 **But if I live in the flesh, this is the fruit of my labor, yet what I shall choose I know not. For I am in a strait between two, having a desire to depart and to be with Christ, which is far better.**

Very frankly, the best thing that can happen to a child of God is for the Lord to come, but the next best thing would be death because he would go to be with the Lord. But you can become rather morbid about this, and I'm afraid some people do. When I had my first cancer surgery a letter came from a lady that said, "I know that everybody's praying that you will get well. I'm praying that the Lord will take you home because to be with Christ is far better." I wrote back and said, "Would you mind letting the Lord decide about this? I want to stay. I'm not anxious to go." And I still want to stay down here as long as I possibly can. I think that is a normal feeling for a child of God.

Paul gives his reason for wanting to stay:

24   **Nevertheless, to abide in the flesh is more needful**
25   **for you. And having this confidence, I know that I shall**
        abide and continue with you all for your furtherance
        and joy of faith.

Paul is practical. He still has work to do. These folk need his ministry. These folk who are always saying, "Oh, if the Lord would only come" should get busy. This is the only place we are going to do any work that is going to count for a reward for Him. What we do in heaven, as far as I can tell, never merits a reward. Down here is the place, the stage on which you and I play our part. I want to stay as long as possible, and I have promised the Lord I'd teach the Word as long as He lets me stay.

26   **That your rejoicing may be more abundant in Jesus**
27   **Christ for me by my coming to you again. Only let**
        your conduct be as it becometh the gospel of Christ,
        that whether I come and see you, or else be absent,
        I may hear of your affairs, that ye stand fast in one
        spirit, with one mind striving together for the faith of
        the gospel.

Notice the words *strife* and *strive*. Paul will tell them later on that there is to be no strife among them. But there should be striving among them. In the word *strive* is the thought of agonizing. We are to agonize together for the faith of the Gospel.

28   **And in nothing terrified by your adversaries, which**
        is to them an evident token of perdition, but to you
29   **of salvation, and that of God. For unto you it is given**
        in the behalf of Christ, not only to believe on him
        but also to suffer for his sake.

Earlier I referred to the suffering of the church in Korea before World War II and during that period. Two very fine missionaries in Korea returned home and were in my church in Pasadena. One evening we were having an informal get-together after the service, and Mrs. Hill gave this verse: "For unto you it is given in the behalf of Christ, not only to believe on him but also to suffer for his sake." She added, "This is the verse that the church in Korea took when persecution broke out." This verse has always meant a great deal to me since that time. It had never impressed me before.

Our Lord must have smiled when He gave John 16:33 to His own yonder in the upper room: "These things I have spoken unto you, that in me ye might have peace." We don't spend much time with this verse today. Just think of the church members who are running to everything trying to find peace. The Lord Jesus categorically has said, "These things I have spoken unto you, that in *me* ye might have peace." The only peace a believer will ever find in this world is in Christ. He'll never find it anywhere else. Notice that He also said, "In the world ye shall have tribulation [trouble]." I often hear this, "I'm having a lot of trouble." You are? Then remember it's just as He said it would be. The child of God is having a lot of trouble in this world. But Jesus adds, "But be of good cheer; I have overcome the world." His victory is our victory if trouble draws us close to the Person of Christ. "For unto you it is given in the behalf of Christ, not only to believe on him but also to suffer for his sake."

30   **Having the same conflict which ye saw in me, and now hear to be in me.**

Paul was the example of suffering in the early church; he is still an example to us today.

PATTERN
FOR CHRISTIAN LIVING

In this second chapter Paul is giving to us probably the greatest doctrinal statement in the New Testament. And it is not ethereal; it was something that walked in shoe leather in the first century in the Roman Empire. You see the mind of Paul—he had the mind of Christ. And Timothy had the mind of Christ because he was like-minded with Paul. Then Epaphroditus, the local pastor in Philippi—his was the work of Christ. He had the mind of Christ, as we shall see.

OTHERS, *verses 1-4*

1   **If there be, therefore any consolation in Christ, if any comfort of love, if any fellowship of the Spirit, if any tender mercies and compassions.**

The **if** that begins this verse is not the *if* of condition. You will find that many times Paul uses *if* as an argument, rather than a condition, and this is how he is using it here. Paul is always logical. If you do not find Paul logical, you are not reading him aright because he is absolutely logical. Now notice his argument; and I'll substitute words for *if*, which will bring out the meaning much better: "Since, therefore, there is consolation in Christ . . ." or "In view of the fact that there *is* consolation in Christ, and since there is comfort of love, and since there is the fellowship of the Spirit, and since there is tenderness and mercy . . ."

Now notice these lovely things. There is consolation in Christ. There is the comfort of love. There is fellowship of the Spirit, and we have talked previously about fellowship. There is tenderness, as we have already seen in the tenderness of Paul and the tenderness of the Philippian Christians toward him. And the mercy—how gracious they were with one another. Now in view of all this, Paul says:

2   Fulfill ye my joy, that ye be like-minded, having the same love, being of one accord, of one mind.

To be **of one accord** does not mean you have to be a duplicate. You don't have to be a Xerox copy of someone else, nor do you have to be a 'yes man.' It does mean that believers should seek a common ground of agreement. You can disagree on minor points of doctrine and still be "of one accord." I have a preacher friend with whom I disagree on almost everything that's not major. We agree on major things, but, boy, we disagree on things that are minor. Yet we are the best of friends, and I have never felt that I should beat him over the head because he disagrees with me. We are to be of one mind, and, as we shall see, that means the mind of Christ.

3   Let nothing be done through strife or vainglory, but in lowliness of mind let each esteem others better than themselves.

Paul, you recall, has said that some were preaching Christ of strife and envy, or vainglory. Here he ways, "Let nothing be done through strife or vainglory." Candidly, if we followed this principle it would solve 90% or maybe even 100% of the problems in churches today.

In lowliness of mind let each esteem others better than themselves would solve the problem in the music department. No one would be saying, "Why in the world did they call on her to sing the solo when I've a much better voice?" It would eliminate the "power struggle" that sometimes goes on among church officers. It would be the solution to a great many problems in our churches, let me tell you!

4   Look not every man on his own things, but every man also on the things of others.

Others—how important this little word is! Why did Christ come from heaven's glory to this earth? Others. Why should we carry the Gospel? Others. We are to think of others. "Let each esteem *others* better than themselves."

THE MIND OF CHRIST—Humble, *verses 5-8*

In this section we find the greatest doctrinal statement in the New Testament. This is known as the *kenosis* theory. It is the emptying of Christ. This gives the humiliation of Christ; there are seven steps that He took downward. I wish I were capable of sketching for you the magnitude of what is being said in these next few verses—of how high He was and how low He came. The billions of light years across known space is nothing compared to the distance He came.

5   **Let this mind be in you, which was also in Christ**
6   **Jesus, who, being in the form of God, thought it not robbery to be equal with God.**

Thought it not robbery to be equal with God is not an adequate translation. Neither does the American Standard Version nor any modern translation convey what is being said here. It is difficult for any of us to get this concept into language. The Lord Jesus Christ was God. It was no effort for Him to be God. He did not go to school and get special training and earn a special degree to become God. He did not work overtime in order to be advanced to the position of God. Nor was it something that, after He was God, He had to hold on to and work hard to keep from losing. When He left heaven's glory to come down to this earth He didn't say to the Father, "Keep Your eye on Gabriel. I think he's after My job." I'm not being irreverent. I'm trying to say that it was something He did not have to hold on to. It *belonged* to Him. He *was* God. Neither did He leave heaven reluctantly. "For the *joy* that was set before Him" (Hebrews 12:2) He endured the cross. He said, "Lo, I come (in the volume of the book it is written of me) to do thy will, I God" (Hebrews 10:7). He came to this earth with joy. He was not releasing something that He wanted to hold on to when He came to this earth.

The *first* step down was when He left heaven's glory.

Now notice the *second* step, and this is where the problem is:

7   **But made himself of no reputation . . .**

Literally, He *emptied* Himself. It is the *kenosis,* the emptying. Of what did the Lord Jesus empty Himself when He came to this earth?

There are those who say He emptied Himself of His deity. All of the Gnostics (like the 57 varieties, they were very numerous in the early church) propounded the first heresy that He emptied Himself of His deity at some time or other.

However, I think we need to put one of the other Prison Epistles with it. In Colossians it ways, "For in him dwelleth all the fullness of the Godhead bodily" (Colossians 2:9). That word "fullness" is *plērōma.* The *kenosis* and the *plērōma.* When Jesus Christ came down to this earth, though He was a little, helpless baby on the bosom of Mary, He could have spoken this universe out of existence. He was God. He was not 99 44/100% God; He was 100% God when He was here. He said to Philip: "Have I been such a long time with you, and yet hast thou not known me, Philip? He that hath seen me hath seen the Father . . ." (John 14:9). In other words, "You've seen God when you've seen Me." The deity of Christ could not be declared in stronger terms than that. We have too many statements that He was God manifest in the flesh to miss His meaning.

> In the beginning was the Word, and the Word was with God, and the Word was God. The same was in the beginning with God. All things were made by him; and without him was not any thing made that was made. . . . And the Word was made [born] flesh, and dwelt among us . . . [John 1:1-3, 14].

When He came down to this earth, He emptied Himself. There was never a moment when He wasn't God. Someone objects, "But He had certain limitations." Yes, but they were only self-limitations, that in which He limited Himself. For instance, He could have turned the stones into bread. If I could have done it, I would have turned that whole rock pile into bread; I would have had a bakery. He could have done that. But there were great limitations He put on Himself. There was never a moment when He wasn't God. And He was not less God because He was man. Yet He emptied Himself of His prerogatives of deity.

The few shepherds and wisemen, and even the multitude of angels were a sorry turnout for the Son of God when He came to this earth. Not only should that crowd have been there, but the whole universe should have been there. All of God's created intelligences should have been there. The hierarchy of Rome should have been there. They should have come from the East—not just a few wisemen—and from the North, South, and West. They should have come from everywhere.

We have to turn to the book of the Revelation to see the universe worshiping Him. John describes the vision given him of heaven in the future when he saw the elders, representing the Church, fall down before Him in worship. Then he saw the angelic host, ten thousand times ten thousand—that's a whole lot of angels! Then John looks around and says, "Oh, my gracious, I didn't see those others!" So he adds, "And thousands of thousands." There is, I think, an infinite number of created intelligences. John said that no man could number them. Why were not *they* at Bethlehem? I'll tell you why. He had laid aside His glory. He laid aside, not His deity, but His prerogatives of deity when He came to this earth. He could walk down the trails yonder in that land; He could go by the Sea of Galilee; He could get weary and sit down at a well. Then they could rebuke Him; they could question Him; they could call Him anything; they could spit in His face; they could crucify Him. Why? He laid aside His prerogatives of deity. Now when He turned in His final report in His Great High Priestly prayer, recorded in John 17 (this is, by the way, the true Lord's Prayer), He prayed to have His glory restored:

> And now, O Father, glorify thou me with thine own
> self with the glory which I had with thee before the world
> was [John 17:5].

He had not laid aside His deity when He came to this earth; He had laid aside His glory. He made Himself of no reputation, and He could be born in a stable back of an inn. The Lord of glory laid aside His prerogatives of deity when He came to this earth.

The *third* step downward in the humiliation of Christ is this:

. . . And [He] took upon him the form of a servant . . .

He could have been born in the palace in Rome. He could have been born a Caesar. But God had already promised that he would be in the line of David. Though coming from the royal line of David, have you ever noticed what Isaiah said concerning him?

> And there shall come forth a rod out of the stem of
> Jesse, and a Branch shall grow out of his roots [Isaiah
> 11:1].

For years that bothered me. I felt like saying, "Isaiah, you should have said, 'Out of the stem of David'." I think if Isaiah could have spoken to me, he would have said, "Oh, how you fellows miss it! The stem comes out of Jesse." When Jesus was born, Israel was under the heel of Rome, the royal line of David was no longer on the throne, but had returned to peasantry. You see, Jesse, the father of King David, was a peasant, a farmer in Bethlehem. And when Jesus was born, the royal line was again in the peasant class. Jesus was born into a poor family. Though He was the Son of David, the stem came out of Jesse. He took upon Himself the form of a servant.

The *fourth* step in His humiliation is this:

. . . And [He] was made in the likeness of men.

This also bothered me for a long time because I couldn't see that being a man was a humiliation. I don't know about you, but I feel very comfortable being a human being. I like it. And I'm delighted to know that in eternity I'm not going to be an angel. As a boy I was sent to Sunday School where we sang that song, "I want to be an angel and with the angels sing." They used to have the meanest bunch of little brats (I was the only good boy in the crowd) stand up and sing, "I want to be an angel." I used to say under my breath, "*I* don't want to be an angel." And I thank God I'll never be an angel. Angels, of course, are a special creation of God. I don't know where the idea came from that human beings would become angels when they went to heaven. I'm thankful that in eternity we'll not be angels. I like the idea of being a man.

But I got to thinking what humiliation it was for Him, who was the second Person of the Godhead, to come down below the position of the angels, and take upon Himself the seed of Abraham. He came in the human line, took upon Himself human flesh, and He was made in the likeness of a man. That, friend, is humiliation. His coming all the way from heaven's glory down to humanity is greater than you and I can comprehend. I do not know how to convey this to you except by a ridiculous illustration.

When we first came to California in 1940, we had the experience of living in a place where the bugs and the ants are not killed off in the wintertime. We got here the first of November, and had not been here long until I found in the kitchen one morning a freeway of ants coming into the sink. They were coming down one side and going back on the other side. Also I found they had discovered the sugar bowl, and they had a freeway in and out of it. I don't know about you, but I don't want ants in the sink and I don't want ants in the sugar bowl. So I began to investigate, and learned that the thing we had to do was to kill them. Now I'm just not sadistic; I'm not brutal; I don't like to kill things. But I began to kill ants. I got ant poison, and we got rid of ants. Then when we moved over to our own home, here were ants. They had found out where we'd moved. So I have a wonderful Christian friend who is in the bug-killing business. He comes to my place twice a year, sprays everything—under the house, under the eaves, the trees—everything, and you can't find an ant on my place. Now I do not know this to be a fact, but I have a notion the ants had a protest meeting around my lot. Maybe they carried banners that read, "Down with McGee. He hates ants!" But, frankly, I don't hate ants. That's not my hang-up at all. If I had some way of communicating with those ants and getting a message to them I'd say, "Look here. I don't hate you. Just stay out of the sugar bowl, and stay out of the sink. I'll put sugar and water outside for you—I'd be glad to do that if you'd just stay outside." But I do not know how to get that message over to the ants—except by becoming an ant. Now suppose that I had the power to become an ant. (If I *could* do it, I would *not* do it because I know some folks who would step on me if I were an ant!) But listen, if I could become an ant—from where I am now down to the position of an ant—that would be humiliation. Wouldn't it? I'd *hate* to become an ant. But, my friend, that is nothing compared to what my Lord did when He left heaven's glory and became a man. When He took upon Himself our humanity, when He was made in the likeness of men.

The *fifth* step in our Lord's humiliation is that He humbled Himself:

8   **And, being found in fashion as a man, he humbled himself . . .**

Notice that it doesn't say He *was* humbled, but that He humbled Himself. When I taped the "Thru the Bible Radio" program for the Gospel of John, I never have been so blessed as I was then as I saw the way He humbled Himself. For instance, when they came out to the Garden to arrest Him, He went forward to meet them, and asked, "Whom seek ye?" They said, "Jesus, of Nazareth." He answered, "I am he." Then for a moment His glory shone forth, and they fell back. They didn't fall forward to worship Him; they fell back because they hated Him and had come out to arrest Him. Then again (imagine a criminal doing this!) He asked, "Whom seek ye." They said, "Jesus, of Nazareth." Again He said, "I am he." What humility to yield Himself into the hands of those men! I've thought the thing through, and I would not have done it. If I'd had the power to deliver myself, I would never have yielded myself to that crowd. Would you? He did. He humbled Himself. "And being found in fashion as a man, he humbled himself."

We today are often humbled, but we don't humble ourselves. Many years ago at a Winona Lake conference, an Englishman was one of the speakers. He was a most dignified gentleman, wore a winged collar and a Prince Albert coat. I wear sport clothes back there—Californian and Hawaiian sport shirts.

One day he said to me, "Ah, Brother McGee, you would not wear that on the platform, would you?"

I said, "Watch me."

He said, "My, I'm shocked." And he was, no question about it.

Well, one afternoon it rained, and in the Billy Sunday Tabernacle a window glass had been broken out so that it had rained in on the platform. In those early days all the speakers in any week would march onto the platform every night, regardless of who was bringing the message. On that particular night I walked behind this dignified, formally dressed Englishman, and when he hit that wet spot on the platform, his feet went out from under him. Oh, how he sprawled! And, you know, everybody laughed. I laughed so hard I had to leave the platform. After I went back and sat down on the platform, I thought I never could quit laughing.

The next night we started in as usual, and he was right ahead of me again. I reached over and said, "Say, it'd be nice to have a repeat performance tonight."

"Oh," he said, "wasn't that humbling!"

Yes, he was humbled, but he did not humble himself. Many times we are humbled. Are we not? But we do not humble ourselves.

The Lord Jesus humbled Himself.

We come now to the *sixth* step in His humiliation:

. . . And [He] became obedient unto death . . .

He became obedient to that awful, frightful thing that is death. Yet He did not *have* to die. He said, "No man taketh it from me, but I lay it down of myself. I have power to lay it down, and I have power to take it again . . ." (John 10:18).

The *seventh* and last step in the humiliation of Christ is that not only did He become obedient unto death, but to the death of the *cross*. "Cursed is everyone that hangeth on a tree" refers to the Mosaic system. The mode of public execution in the Old Testament was by stoning, not by hanging. (Death by crucifixion was the Roman method.) But under the Mosaic system, when a criminal committed a terrible crime and was executed by stoning, then his body would be strung up on a tree for public view because of the enormity of the crime.

> Christ hath redeemed us from the curse of the law,
> being made a curse for us; for it is written, Cursed is
> everyone that hangeth on a tree [Galatians 3:13].

Not only was our Lord obedient to death, but to death by crucifixion. He died a death, and He died on the cross. Why? For others. For you and for me. He came all the way from heaven's glory, came down to this earth. He came to the cross, paying the penalty for your sin and my sin that a holy, righteous God might be able, in love, mercy, and grace, to reach down and save sinners.

The mind of Christ. "Let this mind be in you, which was also in Christ Jesus." This does not come about by imitation, but by im*par*tation. Only the Spirit of God can do this for us. After all, one of the fruits of the Spirit is humility. We try to be meek; we cannot be meek. It is humanly impossible to be meek. It's just not in us at all. Only as the Spirit of God puts the mind of Christ in us is it possible.

THE MIND OF GOD—Exaltation of Christ, *verses 9-11*

As we have seen, there were seven steps downward that He, the Lord of glory, took when He came to this earth. The mind of Christ was a humble mind. Now we come to the mind of God which is the exaltation of Christ. Now we begin the ascension of going back. Here is the *first* step up:

9   Wherefore, God also hath highly exalted him . . .

God intends to exalt Jesus Christ. You and I are living in a world where He is profaned and blasphemed. But it is the intention of God to exalt Him. This is the purpose of God.

The *second* step up is this:

. . . And given him a name which is above every name.

It is a human name. That human name is taken back up, and God intends to exalt it above every other name.

Two thousand years ago the man we know as Jesus of Nazareth did not exist. Somebody says, "Well, I thought He was the eternal God. Yes, two thousand years ago He was the second Person of the Godhead, but He was not Jesus. You see, God could not save when He stayed in heaven—not because there are things impossible with God, but because of the very nature of God. Because He is who He is, He could not remain in heaven and save sinners down here. It was essential for Him to leave heaven's glory and come down to this earth and become Jesus before He could be a Savior.

In Matthew's account we read that Joseph, before the angel Gabriel appeared to him, was about to do a very desperate thing. He didn't intend to stone Mary—the law said that if she were guilty he could stone her—but he was a gentle type man. His thought was to just put her aside. But when he was ready to do this, the angel appeared to him:

> But while he thought on these things, behold, an angel of the Lord appeared unto him in a dream, saying, Joseph, thou son of David, fear not to take unto thee Mary, thy wife; for that which is conceived in her is of the Holy Spirit. And she shall bring forth a son, and thou shalt call his name JESUS; for he shall save his people from their sins [Matthew 1:20,21].

Keep in mind that God said that it is His intention to exalt Jesus and that He has given Him a name that will be above every name, every human name.

Now notice the *third* step of His exaltation.

10   That at the name of Jesus . . .

Before His birth in Bethlehem, the angel ways, "You'll call His name Jesus." Now *Jesus* means "Savior." He will save His people from their sins.

> Now all this was done, that it might be fulfilled which was spoken by the Lord through the prophet, saying, Behold, the virgin shall be with child, and shall bring

> forth a son, and they shall call his name Immanuel, which,
> being interpreted, is God with us [Matthew 1:22, 23].

Can you show me any place in the Bible where He was called Immanuel? When I entered the ministry, I had no problem with "Behold a virgin shall conceive." Since He is God, how else could He get into the human family except by a miraculous birth? But the thing that did cause a problem in this verse was, "He shall be called Immanuel" because I couldn't find any place where they called Him Immanuel. "Well, then," you may say, "that prophecy was not fulfilled." Oh, my friend, this is one of the most wonderful fulfillments of prophecy you can imagine. The angel said, "Call Him Jesus because He'll save His people from their sins." Now think through this. You couldn't call me *Jesus*—I can't even save myself. Neither would it be accurate to call you *Jesus* because you can't save yourself. You see, all of us are on the same ship today. The human family is on a sinking ship, and it's going down. If there is to be a Savior, He's got to come from the outside. There are those today who want to throw out a lifeline. It is like a ship that is sinking. Somebody on the top deck says to those down in the steerage, "Let me throw you a lifeline." A man looks up and says, "Aren't you on the top deck?"

"Yes."

"Isn't the top deck going down too?"

"Yes."

"Well, then, if you pull me up there all you'd be doing is keeping my feet out of water about five minutes longer."

You see, the rope has to come from some other place than the human ship. No human being can be a Savior. "You shall call His name *Jesus* because He is going to save His people from their sins." How can He save His people from their sins? Because He will be Immanuel, God with us. That little Baby who came yonder to Bethlehem is God with us. He took upon Himself, not the likeness of angels, but our humanity. He is Immanuel, God with us. And because He is that, He can be called Jesus. And, friend, nobody else can properly be called *Jesus*.

Now God says, "I'm going to exalt the name which was given to Him when He came to earth above every other name. Now notice the *fourth* step of His exaltation:

> **That at the name of Jesus every knee should bow,**
> **of things in heaven . . .**

And the *fifth* step:

> **. . . And things in earth . . .**

And the *sixth* step:

> **. . . And things under the earth.**

This verse is used by the Restitutionalists to support their theory that ultimately everybody will be saved. We had a spokesman of this cult in Los Angeles for many years. He made the statement that Judas Iscariot and the devil would be walking down the streets of heaven together because ultimately all would be saved. Of course it was unfortunate that he used this verse because when you compare it with Colossians 1:20, you see its true meaning. The subject in the Philippians passage is the lordship of Jesus. God has highly exalted Him, that at the name of Jesus every knee must bow, in heaven, in earth, and under the earth. That is, even hell will have to bow to Him because He is the Lord. He is God. But merely bowing does not imply salvation. Colossians clarifies this:

> And, having made peace through the blood of his cross,
> by him to reconcile all things unto himself—by him, I
> say, whether they be things in earth, or things in heaven
> [Colossians 1:20].

This verse is not talking about lordship, but about Christ's reconciling work, His redemptive work. And what was reconciled? What was redeemed? Was hell included? No. The things *under the earth* are not mentioned here. Why? Because this verse is talking about redemption, and there is no redemption in hell. By putting these two verses together it is clear that those in hell who bow to Jesus are merely acknowledging His lordship. "That at the name of Jesus every knee should bow, of things in heaven, and things in earth, and things under the earth."

Here now is the *seventh* and final step of Christ's exaltation:

11   And that every tongue should confess that Jesus Christ is Lord, to the glory of God, the Father.

According to Scripture even the demons know who He is. In the Gospels, you remember, it is recorded that demons recognized Him and confessed that He was the Son of God. They knew who He was. A lot of folk today do not know who He is, but *they* did. Even hell itself will have to acknowledge His lordship. Those who hated Him, those who turned their backs upon Him, those who rejected Him (it's hard to understand the hatred that some have for the Lord Jesus Christ today), will finally have to acknowledge the lordship of this One who came to earth over 1900 years ago.

This is a tremendous section. The Lord of glory came all the way down to this earth. He went to the cross and died a redemptive, vicarious, substitutionary death for you and for me. He did this for *others*. He did this to reveal the love of God. It was a display of His love which no created intelligence of God knew about before. They knew about His wisdom, they knew something about His power, they knew something about His greatness and glory, but they knew nothing about His love until Jesus Christ came to this earth and died for sinners. In the book of Revelation John sketches for us that great worship scene of the future in heaven when the created intelligences join with the Church in universal adoration:

> And every creature that is in heaven, and on the earth, and under the earth, and such as are in the sea, and all that are in them heard I saying, Blessing, and honor, and glory, and power be unto him that sitteth upon the throne, and unto the Lamb forever and ever [Revelation 5:13].

When Jesus Christ came to this earth, He bore the curse of sin. And he's been blasphemed; He's been rejected in this world. You and I today are living in the day of His rejection. But God says that one day He is going to exalt Him, and that every created intelligence, everything that has breath, is going to acknowledge His lordship. They will *have* to acknowledge it. But during these days of His rejection, we have the freedom to *bow* to Him and call Him our Savior and Lord.

I was talking to some of these young folk who are in rebellion—and I sort of feel like joining them in the rebellion. But I asked one young fellow, "Why do you dress as you do?"

"I'm expressing my freedom!"

"Would your crowd accept you if you got rid of those rags and put on regular clothes?"

"No, they wouldn't."

"Here you are looking for freedom, and you don't even know what freedom is! You *have* to dress like that if you're going to run with your crowd. That's not freedom."

"Well, what do you think freedom is?"

And I told him about the real freedom that Christ gives. And the glorious freedom I have in these days of His rejection to acknowledge Him and bow to Him.

This is the mind of God, to exalt Christ.

MIND OF PAUL—Things of Christ, *verses 12-18*

While we need to exalt Christ, let's remember that His mind was a humble mind. Now let's see how this worked in the lives of others. Let's look now at the mind of Paul.

12   Wherefore, my beloved, as ye have always obeyed, not as in my presence only but now much more in my absence, work out your own salvation with fear and trembling.

In other words, "I'm in prison. I'm not able to come to you. I think I may be freed, but I don't know. And since I'm not there with you, you work out your own salvation." He meant, I think, that which concerned their Christian life, that which concerned the work of the church. "Work out your own salvation with fear and trembling."

13   For it is God who worketh in you both to will and to do of his good pleasure.

When a preacher read this passage in a service, a little girl said in a stage whisper to her mother, "Mommy, you can't work it out unless it's been worked in, can you?" She was quite accurate. A great many people say that salvation means there is something you have to work at, something you have to do. My friend, you must have it before you can work it out. You work out your salvation which has first been worked in—"for it is God which worketh in you both to will and to do of His good pleasure."

14   Do all things without murmurings and disputings.

This verse ought to be put up in different places in the church. I do not think we realize how disputings and murmurings hurt the cause of Christ. Christian work should not be done with murmurings and disputings regardless of how great a work it might be. Murmurings and disputings absolutely nullify it.

15   **That ye may be blameless and harmless, children of God, without rebuke, in the midst of a crooked and perverse nation; among whom ye shine as lights in the world.**

Harmless—you remember the Lord Jesus said something about being harmless as a dove but wise as a serpent. We are not to harm the cause of Christ with our murmurings and disputings.

Blameless—in other words, we are not to be guilty if we are accused. Shortly after I became pastor in downtown Los Angeles, I talked with Dr. Jim McGinlay, whom I always considered to be a great preacher. Knowing something of the problems of a large church, he asked me how I liked being pastor of the Church of the Open Door.

"Fine," I said, "but I find myself in the unique position of not being able to protect myself. When I hear certain charges made, I can't answer them."

In his Scotch accent he said, "Just thank God and be sure the charges made against you are not true."

I have often thought of that. We cannot escape, friend, being gossiped about, but when we hear the accusation, we can just thank God it is not true. As God's children our lives are to be blameless, harmless, without rebuke.

When we go out at night we see the stars up there. When God looks down on this dark world, He sees those who are His own as little lights down here. The children sing "This Little Light of Mine." Well, my friend, that's exactly what it is. Paul says, **"Among whom ye shine as lights in the world."** As the stars are up there, we are down here.

16   **Holding forth the word of life, that I may rejoice in the day of Christ that I have not run in vain, neither labored in vain.**

Remember that these believers in Philippi were very close to the heart of Paul because they were his converts.

Now notice here the mind of Paul:

17   **Yea, and if I be offered upon the sacrifice and service of your faith, I joy, and rejoice with you all.**

This has reference to the drink offering. When you go back to Leviticus where the instructions are given for the five offerings, you find no instructions about the drink offering, none whatsoever. But in reading Leviticus you discover that on the peace offering they were to pour a drink offering. It was a most unusual offering in that it had nothing to do with redemption; it had nothing to do with the Person of Christ. They would bring in one of those bags of wine and just pour it on a burnt offering, a peace offering—not on a sin offering or trespass offering—but on the others. When it was poured on a sacrifice which was being consumed by fire, what happened to it? It would just disappear, go up in steam. Now Paul is saying, "I want my life to be poured out like a drink offering on the offering of Christ." What will happen to it? It will just go up in steam. You see, Paul did not want anything named for him after he was gone. He was not looking for any kind of fame. He simply wanted his life to be poured out on the offering of Christ, that Christ might receive all the honor and the glory. This man had the mind of Christ, you see. I can think of nothing that is higher than that.

When you read down through the history of the church, you will find quite a company of men and women whose lives have been poured out as a sacrifice. I think of a missionary to Venezuela, old Al Tuggy. He was a missionary who, when he retired, wouldn't come home. He stayed in Venezuela. And actually he didn't retire. When I was in Venezuela, and I'll always appreciate this, he took me in his car around to different places. One day we went up through those coffee haciendas, way up to see a Christian man whom he had led to the Lord when he first went down there as a missionary. He spoke Spanish better than English. As he'd be talking to me he'd stop and say, "How do you say that in English? I can say it in Spanish but not in English." He'd been down there so long. And he had a little home there at Las Delicias on the side of a mountain. Not long after I returned home here came a cablegram informing me that Brother Al Tuggy had gone home to be with the Lord. He had worked that day in the shop, had gone home for lunch, then on the way down had a heart attack. One of the Venezuelan Christians had a plot of ground, and he said, "I want Mr. Tuggy buried right here." After they had buried him, these Venezuelans came around to Mrs. Tuggy and said, "Now he's really ours. He came down here as a missionary and we learned to love him, but we always thought someday he would go back to the United States. He didn't go back, and now he belongs to us." His life was like Paul's, it was a drink offering.

just poured out down there. Few have ever heard of Al Tuggy and the missionary work he did down there in the jungles of Venezuela, but he was mightily used of God. There is a great army of folk like him whose lives were just a drink offering poured out. Perhaps nobody knows about it down here, but God knows about it because it ascended to Him.

18 **For the same cause also do ye joy, and rejoice with me.**

Notice the joy that is in this section.

THE MIND OF TIMOTHY—Like-minded with Paul, *verses 19-24*

19 **But I trust in the Lord Jesus to send Timothy shortly unto you, that I also may be of good comfort, when I know your state. For I have no man like-minded, who will naturally care for your state.**

Timothy was like-minded with Paul. That was a marvelous relationship. I do not know why it is true, but it is very difficult in Christian work to get loyal workers. In the past few years I have talked with more than 100 pastors in this country who have found disloyalty in their staffs—and it's generally in a Christian Education director—which has brought tragedy to him and to his church. It is hard to find workers in the Lord's work who know anything about loyalty. I have brought this fact to the attention of seminary professors. I have suggested, "Why in the world don't you drop one of your Greek or Hebrew courses and teach loyalty? That is something that needs to be taught today." Obviously Paul had problems with it because he said, "I haven't any other who is like-minded as Timothy is." Now what is meant by being like-minded? Paul had the mind of Christ, and Timothy had the mind of Christ. And when two men have the mind of Christ, my friend, they can work together regardless of the circumstances.

21 **For all seek their own, not the things which are Jesus Christ's. But ye know the proof of him, that, as a son with the father, he hath served with me in the gospel. Him, therefore, I hope to send presently, as soon as I shall see how it will go with me.**

Paul expected to be released from prison. There is nothing in the scripture that indicates he was released because the book of Acts ends before that took place. However, there is good tradition that Paul was released from prison and had quite an itinerant ministry after this, although it is not recorded in Scripture. His ministry ended yonder in Rome, as far as the record is concerned, because the church was to go on under different leadership and the ministry of other men.

24 **But I trust in the Lord that I also myself shall come shortly.**

And I believe that he did. Personally, I think that Paul went to Spain, and probably to Great Britain. My reason for thinking he went to Spain is that he wrote to the Romans, "Whenever I take my journey into Spain, I will come to you; for I trust to see you in my journey . . ." (Romans 15:24). Also in his second letter to Timothy, his swan song, he wrote, ". . . I have finished my course . . ." (2 Timothy 4:7). In other words, Paul touched all the bases. I think he went to Spain; I think he went all the way around the track because at the end of his life he said he had finished his course.

MIND OF EPAPHRODITUS—The Work of Christ, *verses 25-30*

25 **Yet I thought it necessary to send to you Epaphroditus, my brother and companion in labor, and fellow soldier, but your messenger, and him that ministered to my need.**

Now, isn't this lovely? Paul always has something good to say about the local preacher: "He's my brother, he's my companion in labor, he's my fellow soldier—but your messenger—and he ministered to my needs."

26
27 **For he longed after you all, and was full of heaviness, because ye had heard that he had been sick. For, indeed, he was sick near unto death, but God had mercy on him; and not on him only, but on me also, lest I should have sorrow upon sorrow.**

Paul is sending him back to Philippi.

28
29 **I sent him, therefore, the more eagerly that, when ye see him again, ye may rejoice, and that I may be the less sorrowful. Receive him, therefore, in the Lord with all gladness, and hold such in reputation.**

How gracious Paul is with this preacher from Philippi.

30   **Because, for the work of Christ, he was near unto death, not regarding his life, to supply your lack of service toward me.**

In other words, "Epaphroditus, your pastor who was here, was so sick he almost died for the cause of Christ." Epaphroditus has the mind of Christ.

Picture now these men in the first century. They were in pagan Rome—and, believe me, Rome was pagan. There was not a power in that day that could protest against Rome. This man Paul was a Roman citizen, and he could walk down the streets of Rome, or any city in the Roman Empire, among all that paganism, and still have the mind of Christ. Timothy, who was with him, his companion, walked down these same roads, and he had the mind of Christ. And Epaphroditus, a preacher from way over yonder in Philippi, who risked his life to come to Paul in Rome, and went back on shipboard with pagans and heathens—he had the mind of Christ. My friend, if these men could have the mind of Christ in the first century, today in the twentieth century right where we are now, you and I can have the mind of Christ. Not by imitation, but by yielding to Him can the Spirit of God produce in our own lives the mind of Christ. Oh, how desperately that is needed in our day!

PRIZE
FOR CHRISTIAN LIVING

The philosophy of Christian living was given to us in Chapter 1: "For me to live Christ, and to die gain." Chapter 2 outlines the pattern for Christian living: "Let this mind be in you, which was also in Christ Jesus"—and that is impartation, not imitation. Now we come to the prize for Christian living.

PAUL CHANGED HIS BOOKKEEPING
SYSTEM OF THE PAST, *verses 1-9*

1   **Finally, my brethren, rejoice in the Lord. To write the same things to you, to me indeed is not irksome but for you it is safe.**

Finally, my brethren . . . gives us the impression that Paul is coming to the conclusion of this Epistle. When he gets midway in Chapter 4 he will say it again: "Finally, brethren . . ." I think Paul intended to bring this letter to a conclusion at this point, but the Spirit of God prompted him to go on. So, friend, when your pastor on Sunday morning announces the last point of his sermon, then continues on and on and on, don't find fault with him—he's being 'scriptural'—this is actually what Paul is doing here!

In view of all that was said in the first two chapters about having the mind of Christ, he says, "Finally, my brethren, rejoice in the Lord

51

. . ." Here were three men, Paul, Timothy, and Epaphroditus, when Christianity was just beginning, who had the mind of Christ. And, my, how God blessed those early years of the Church. After 200 years there were millions of Christians in the Roman Empire. Nothing has ever grown and flourished as the Church did amid the fires of persecution. No wonder Paul can begin this chapter by saying, "Rejoice in the Lord." This man Paul had a tremendous hope.

To write the same things to you, to me indeed is not irksome but for you it is safe. You remember that Paul wrote to the Corinthians, "I can't write unto you as unto spiritual, but as unto carnal. I have to write to you like this because you are carnal, baby Christians." In contrast to them, the Philippians were matured spiritually. And they loved the Apostle Paul and he loved them and felt close to them. So he says, "To write the same things to you, to me indeed is not irksome but for you it is safe." That is, "You'll understand."

2   Beware of dogs, beware of evil workers, beware of the concision.

Beware of dogs—what does he mean by *dogs?* Are these the kind of dogs that try to chew up the mailman? I have a dog that would love to eat our mailman. I don't know why he picks on him. I have tried to explain to him that our mailman is a lovely fellow, but he doesn't believe me. Is Paul's warning against dogs, the four-legged kind? No. He is warning against the two-legged kind. I think he had in mind the same thing expressed by Isaiah:

> His watchmen are blind; they are all ignorant, they
> are all dumb dogs, they cannot bark; sleeping, lying down,
> loving to slumber [Isaiah 56:10].

Isaiah is warning his people against false prophets, who fail to warn the children of Israel. The Northern Kingdom had gone into captivity because the false prophets had given them a false security which wasn't warranted. And God was warning the Southern Kingdom that unless they turned back to Him they would be carried into captivity also. God speaks of the false prophets as "dumb dogs"—they won't speak out, won't tell it like it is. There is a danger today in the pulpit of not telling it like it is. And I think this is Paul's meaning here: Beware of dogs, beware of those who are not declaring the full counsel of God.

Beware of evil workers—now this is another group, that would actually abuse them and use them.

Beware of the concision. The concision are the Judaizers, the legalists. Notice that Paul changes the word *circumcision (peritomē)* to "concision" *(katatomē)*. Why does he say it like that?

3   **For we are the circumcision, who worship God in the spirit, and rejoice in Christ Jesus, and have no confidence in the flesh.**

Elsewhere he says that true circumcision is of the heart by the new birth—not merely an external observance, but a heart attitude toward God.

We . . . worship God in the spirit, and rejoice in Christ Jesus. This is the second time he has used that word *rejoice.* God wants you to rejoice, friend. Have you ever noticed that God appointed His people Israel seven *feast* days in the year—not one of them was a fast day. In substance God said, "I don't want you to come into My presence with a long, pious face. I want you to come into my presence with rejoicing." Again and again the psalmist says, "Let us come into the House of the Lord with joy, with praise, with thanksgiving." That should be the attitude of the child of God.

And have no confidence in the flesh refers to the old nature. We have no confidence in our old nature. Rather, we trust Christ alone. We do not look to ourselves for salvation at all. You see, the legalizers followed Paul around; that is, they would come to a group of believers after Paul had been there and spread their false teaching. They had followed him into the Galatian country, and their false teaching is the subject of Paul's Epistle to the Galatians. They would circulate a report that went something like this: "Brother Paul says that we can't have confidence in the flesh. Do you know why he says that? Because Paul personally has nothing of which to boast. Oh, yes, he's an apostle, but he is a Johnny-come-lately, he was not one of the original twelve. Now others may have something to boast of, but actually Paul has nothing. He says *you* can't have confidence in the flesh because *he* can't have confidence in the flesh."

Now Paul answers that. He beats them to the draw, by the way.

4   **Though I might also have confidence in the flesh. If any other man thinketh that he hath reasons for which he might trust in the flesh, I more.**

I had always felt that Nicodemus was probably the acme of Pharisaism. But this verse lets me know that Paul was in the top bracket as a Pharisee. Nicodemus was religious to his fingertips; he was a leader, a ruler of the Jews, a Pharisee. When he came to Jesus with questions, our Lord did not criticize him from the standpoint of his profession. In contrast, later when other Pharisees came to Him, He called them hypocrites. He never called Nicodemus a hypocrite because he was not. He was religious to his fingertips. But Paul was even more religious than Nicodemus. He says, "If any other man thinketh that he hath reasons for which he might trust in the flesh, I more." I believe that Paul the apostle, when he was Saul of Tarsus, was the most religious man that ever has been on this earth.

Now he is going to list seven things in which men trust, and in which he trusted at one time. This is religion—if anybody could have been saved by religion, Saul of Tarsus could have been saved by religion. As he enumerates these seven things, notice that these are seven things that people boast of today. Now if you are boasting of any of these, let's understand one thing: None of them have anything to do with your salvation. The 'religion of the flesh' is very prevalent in America today. These are things you hear people boasting of, but none of them can save you, although some of them are good things.

**5   Circumcised the eighth day, of the stock of Israel, of
        the tribe of Benjamin, an Hebrew of the Hebrews; as
6   touching the law, a Pharisee; concerning zeal, perse-
        cuting the church; touching the righteousness which
        is in the law, blameless.**

(1) **Circumcised the eighth day.** This is a basic rite, not only of the Mosaic system, but it goes back to Abraham. When Paul says that he was circumcised the eighth day, he is making it clear that he had godly parents. It was his religious parents who saw to it the rite was performed. You remember that it was said of the Lord Jesus that on the eighth day He was brought into the Temple and circumcised. It was a very important rite in the religion of Israel.

It is wonderful to have godly parents, but you'll never get to heaven tied to your mama's apron strings. Neither will your father's faith save you. The fact that I did not have godly parents gave me an inferior feeling when I went to seminary. Practically every boy in the class I was in gave testimony of being led to Christ by his mother. I didn't start off that way. I always felt it was wonderful to have had godly parents, but I found out that a lot of folk with godly parents don't fare so well in this life because they are depending on the religion of their parents.

(2) **Of the stock of Israel.** And, believe me, that was something to boast of. In the books of Ezra and Nehemiah there are the records of certain men who were disqualified as priests because they could not give their genealogy. They had to know who they were. Paul knew who he was: "I'm an Israelite."

There are a lot of people today who feel that church membership is essential to salvation. If you are saved, you ought to belong to a church, but church membership just doesn't have a thing to do with your salvation.

When Paul said, "I am of the stock of Israel," one button popped off his vest because that was something to boast of.

(3) **Of the tribe of Benjamin.** That's like saying, "I belong to one of the first families." That doesn't count in California, but in the South where I was raised, you'd better belong to one of the first families. If you don't, you will find yourself at the end of the line. So when Paul said he belonged to the tribe of Benjamin, that was pretty important.

Benjamin, you remember, was the favorite son of old Jacob. When Joseph was down in Egypt, and when the other sons went down to Egypt to get grain because of the famine, they came back to their father and said, "We can't go back without our younger brother." Old Jacob said, "Why did you tell the man you had a younger brother?" Finally when the famine grew and again they were out of grain, Jacob said, "You'll have to go back to Egypt." They said, "We'll have to take Benjamin." "Well," he said, "if I let him go, let's understand one thing: if anything happens to him it will bring me down to an untimely death." And that boy was really protected by his brothers. Judah was willing to put his life on the line for him. As a result of this, the tribe of Benjamin became the favorite tribe. After Israel became a nation and was looking for a king, where did they go? They went to the tribe of Benjamin and chose Saul. Probably this Saul of Tarsus was named after King Saul. So, you see, Paul could say with pride, "I'm of the tribe of Benjamin."

(4) **An Hebrew of the Hebrews**—when he said that two buttons popped off his vest, because it meant he was a leader. He was in the highest strata of the religious circle. Today a lot of people like to be leaders in the church, like to have position.

(5) As touching the law, a Pharisee. Now the Pharisees represented the best in Israel. They were a religio-political party, and their aim was to establish the kingdom. They were very much interested in that. I think that is the reason they sent Nicodemus to see Jesus. Their thinking was, *Here's a prophet come out of Galilee. If he'll just let us hitch our wagon to his star, we'll go places because we know how to manipulate Rome.* Nicodemus wanted to talk to Him about the kingdom. And, you remember, the Lord Jesus corrected his thinking at the very outset, "Verily, verily, I say unto thee, Except a man be born again, he cannot see the kingdom of God." In other words, "You are not even in a position to talk about it." But the Pharisees as a party, thought that by political manipulation they could bring in the kingdom.

Let me say, and say it kindly, that this is the very heart-blood of the Roman Catholic Church. Had you ever stopped to think about it? At this writing the Pope has made a trip. Did he talk to anybody about salvation? No. He talked about world peace and what we ought to be doing to achieve it. Do you know why? They are trying to build the kingdom here upon this earth. Now Protestantism has gone off on this tangent also, and they put the emphasis on political issues.

So, Paul as a Pharisee, represented the best in Israel. In religion he was fundamental; in politics he was extremely nationalistic.

(6) Concerning zeal, persecuting the church. He was zealous. And zeal without knowledge, as someone has said, is a dangerous thing. He thought he was doing God's will when he persecuted the church. Probably Jesus Christ never again has had an enemy like Saul of Tarsus. As I have said, I think he was present at the crucifixion. He was in the environs of Jerusalem, in the school of Gamaliel. Zealous as he was, I can't believe the man would stay at home the day they crucified Jesus! The Pharisees were the ones, you recall, who were in the cheering section that shot out the lip and ridiculed our Lord as He hung on the cross; and then sat down and watched Him die. Saul, I'm confident, was in that crowd. I believe he had that in mind when later on he said, "I'm the chiefest of sinners. I persecuted the church, thinking I was doing God's will." He had zeal without knowledge.

(7) Touching the righteousness which is in the law, blameless. Notice he does not say he was perfect; he said he was blameless. Did Paul mean that he had actually reached the state of sinless perfection? No, he made it clear that he had not: ". . . I had not known sin but by the law; for I had not known coveting, except the law had said,

Thou shalt not covet" (Romans 7:7). He made it clear that he could put the first nine commandments down on his life and he could stand before God and say, "I have kept these." (I doubt if you or I could say, "I have kept the first nine commandments"! Believe me, that was something of which to boast.) But when he came to that tenth commandment: "Thou shalt not covet," that got him. "I broke that one," he said. "I coveted."

Now, if he had kept his mouth shut, nobody would have ever known. Covetousness is a sin you can commit without anybody knowing what you are doing. If you lie, you'll have to tell half a dozen more to cover that one up, and somebody will catch you in it for sure; if you steal you'll get caught with the goods sooner or later; you can't commit adultery without somebody knowing it; if you murder, you have a *corpus delicti* on your hands. But you can covet in public view and nobody will know it. Now Paul did not try to cover it up like a lot of us do today; he confessed it. He brought the sacrifice into the Temple for that sin to make things right before God, so that "touching the righteousness which is in the law, [he] was blameless"—not sinless, but blameless.

In passing, let me say that the sin of covetousness which Paul says "slew" him, slays a great many of us today. It is America's great sin. It is idolatry, modern idolatry. It's like this: "Oh, look, the Joneses have a new car. It's a new Wompuscat! My! Guess we'll have to trade in our old bus." What is that? Covetousness. And I tell my wife when she goes window-shopping that it is the most polite, the cleanest, way to covet I know anything about. The very act of coveting is in the warp and woof of the being of man. Our environment lends itself to a life of desire.

Paul brought his sin out in the open and confessed it before God. Confession of sin is one of the most neglected areas of Christian living today. No wonder we have so many weak Christians! They have unconfessed sin in their lives. We need to deal with our sin, friend, and confess it before God.

Regarding the law, Paul was a super-saint. He says, "If any other man thinketh that he hath reasons for which he might trust in the flesh, I more."

But notice what happened to him:

7   **But what things were gain to me, those I counted loss for Christ.**

His encounter with Christ on the Damascus Road was the greatest revolution that ever takes place—and it takes place every time a person comes to Christ. You see, Paul had a debit. His loss was Christ. He hated Him. He was traveling on the road to Damascus for the purpose of arresting Christians who were His followers. Christ was a debit and a loss to him. Over on the credit side, that which was gain, Paul had the seven religious credits which we have seen. On the Damascus Road he met Christ. What happened? What was a gain to him became a loss; what was a loss became a gain. In substance he says, "Those religious credits I had—I no longer trust in them. That which was my loss—who was Christ—I now trust Him only." This, my friend, is conversion. It is salvation when a man turns *from* religion and trusting the things of the flesh *to* trusting Christ, only Christ. That's revolutionary.

To illustrate, suppose I were to come home from a trip, go down to our favorite department store and say, "My wife has been doing some shopping here, and I want to pay the bill."

Suppose the bookkeeper says, "Oh, Dr. McGee, since you've been gone, we've changed our bookkeeping system. What was a gain is a loss; what was a loss is a gain. A debit is a credit, and credits are debits. Instead of you owing us, we owe you, and we have a check for you." My friend, that would be revolutionary! What would it do to the economy of this country today? If debits became credits and credits became debits it would bring a revolution in the economy of the world.

This is exactly what happened to the Apostle Paul. "That which was gain to me became a loss. I no longer trusted religion; I came to trust Christ, Christ only." His life was absolutely turned upside down and right side up and inside out.

Between verses 7 and 8 there is a time lapse. In fact, I think that lapse extends all the way through this man's life from his conversion to the time he is writing this Epistle. Now he has been a missionary for many years, he has made three great missionary journeys. Now, in a Roman prison he says:

8   **Yea doubtless, and I count all things but loss for the excellency of the knowledge of Christ Jesus, my Lord; for whom I have suffered the loss of all things, and do count them but refuse that I may win Christ.**

In other words, "I haven't changed my mind down through the years. I still have the same faith that I had at the beginning."

It is well for every believer, regardless of who he is, to make periodic inventory. The world takes an annual inventory, why shouldn't the Christian? Where am I spiritually? What do I really believe? Am I progressing or regressing? You recall that our Lord wrote to the church at Ephesus, which was the finest church of all, "Nevertheless, I have somewhat against thee, because thou art leaving thy best love" (Revelation 2:4). How about you? Do you remember when you first came to Christ what a thrill it was? Do you have that same thrill today? Paul said, "I'm as thrilled as I was the day I met Jesus Christ on the Damascus Road. I count all things *right now* loss for the excellency of the knowledge of Christ Jesus, my Lord."

My Lord he calls Him. He is writing, as we shall see, to a colony of Rome which was Philippi. And they never called Caesar *Lord* until he was deified. That's interesting. Paul says, "Christ Jesus is my Lord. He's the One whom I worship."

In the Authorized Version the word **refuse** is *dung*—and I think that is a better word for it. Paul is saying about those things that were gain to him, "I flush them down! I don't trust them any more. And the One whom I hated above all else, Jesus Christ, I now trust Him *only* for my salvation."

This is salvation. You get saved when you cease trusting these things of the flesh and trust Christ and Christ alone. Dr. Lewis Sperry Chafer used to put it like this: "I want to so trust Christ that when I come before Him some day, and He should say to me, 'Lewis, why are you here?' I would say, 'I trusted You as my Savior.' If He should say, 'Well, that was very fine of you, but don't you have something else?' 'No, I don't. I did not trust anything else.' 'Well, now, you were president of a seminary. Wouldn't you like to mention that?' 'No.' 'You were very religious.' 'No, I don't want to mention that.' 'You did many good things.' 'Yes, but I never trusted those things.' 'Well, I'm sorry, I cannot accept you.'" Dr Chafer said, "I want to so trust Christ that I would say to Him, 'I only trusted You.' And I'd turn and walk away."

That is what it means to trust Christ as your Savior—I don't know of a better way to put it.

"That I may win Christ"—Paul is saying, "I'm still out on the race course, pressing toward the mark for the prize of the high calling of God in Christ Jesus. I'm still moving out there. I'm still working for a prize."

**9   And be found in him, not having mine own right-
        eousness, which is of the law, but that which is through
        the faith of Christ, the righteousness which is of God
        by faith.**

This is the verse that came to John Bunyan, as he walked through the corn fields one night. He said, "I did not see myself as only a sinner, but as sin from the crown of my head to the sole of my feet. I knew that John Bunyan could not stand in the presence of God." Then this verse came to him: "And be found in him, not having mine own right-eousness which is of the law, but that which is through the faith of Christ, the righteousness which is of God by faith." John Bunyan said that he reached out by faith and received Christ. What happened to Paul the apostle, happened to John Bunyan, and it has happened to millions of men and women down through the ages. It is a revolution of soul that completely changes the bookkeeping system. What was gain becomes loss; what was loss becomes eternal gain.

PAUL CHANGED HIS PURPOSE
FOR THE PRESENT, *verses 10-19*

In this section we see that Paul has changed his entire present outlook, and his entire purpose has changed. Being saved by faith may give the impression that there is no motivation for conduct and works. Paul dissipates that notion in this section. He exhibits an effort and energy derived from the Holy Spirit which is far greater than any legal effort. Under the law he would go to Damascus to stamp out the followers of Christ. Under the grace-faith system, he will go to the end of the earth to make followers of Christ and to witness for Him.

**10   That I may know him, and the power of his resur-
        rection, and the fellowship of his sufferings, being
        made conformable unto his death.**

The power of the resurrection—the power that raised Jesus from the dead. Paul says, "I want that power to work in my life." Someone has given a very free interpretation—not a translation—that brings out the thought of the Apostle Paul in this passage:

Ever since I saw Christ in the glory of God, I have considered nothing else as worth living for. He has so won my heart that nothing now counts with me but the blessedness of knowing Him, of being completely identified with Him both in life and in death, yes, and beyond death. I would not stand before God in a righteousness of my own now if I could. I desire only to be found in Him. I long only to know Him more intimately. Let the suffering involved be what it may, I would even die as He died . . . if need be, any way that He may choose, that at last, whatever way may lead me to it, I shall attain unto the great rapture of all saints at His coming, the glorious 'out resurrection' from among the dead. This for me will be the goal attained which has been for so long before my soul, for then I shall be so completely identified with Him, who has won my heart to Himself, that I shall be like Him forever and with Him through all the ages to come.

Or, to paraphrase it a little differently, Paul is saying "Now that I've come to Christ, He has become the object of my affections. I live for Him, and I am longing for the day that I'll come into His presence. I am willing to suffer for Him. In fact, I have suffered for Him, and it has drawn me closer to Him."

The fellowship of his sufferings is something the saints today do not like. We don't want pain. We criticize our younger generation for taking drugs, but some of us have been taking pain relievers for years. And don't misunderstand me—I'm not pointing the finger at you. When I have a tooth filled, I don't want to feel it. I want to avoid pain. When the anesthetist came to me in the hospital to talk with me about the anesthesia for the next day's surgery, I said, "There's just one thing I want to ask of you. I do not want to *know* when I leave this room and when I come back. Will you see to that?" He said "I'll see to it," and he did. We live in that kind of a day, don't we? We do not want pain. But I am convinced that there is no other way of being drawn close to the Person of Christ except through suffering. The sweetest saints I meet today are those who are suffering, or have some great handicap to get over. My friend, this is something to think about in these days.

Let me share just an excerpt of a letter from a woman who is in real trouble: "I'm asking that you pray for healing for me. Within one year I lost my mother under tragic circumstances; my husband went broke and we lost our home; and I was found to have cancer which necessitated the removal of both breasts—all this while trying to raise three wonderful children. Truly God's grace is sufficient, but I need prayer for courage. The other side of the family are Unity students, so I understand Job and his miserable comforters. Unity feels you *think* yourself into cancer, so they have simply stayed away from me. But, oh, what I am learning in the furnace!" Then she writes of how she has been drawn closer to Christ through these experiences.

Now let's be frank. Would you be willing to go through that to be drawn closer to Him? I'll be very candid with you, I told Him, "No, I don't want cancer." And I don't. It's a monster—I hate it. But I had no choice, and Christ has become more real to me since I had cancer than He ever was before. I am convinced that "the fellowship of His sufferings" means exactly what it says. Christ suffered and bled on that cross for me, and I'll never have to suffer like that for the penalty of my sins, but if I'm to have close fellowship with Him, I'll have to suffer down here. I have letters from folk who are suffering—honestly, what they are going through is devastating. I don't see how they bear up under it. Yet through it they are being made sweet, and are being drawn close to the Lord.

11   **If by any means I might attain unto the resurrection of the dead.**

If does not express doubt that the Apostle Paul would participate in the Rapture. But he is in Rome at this time, in prison, and mad Nero is on the throne. He does not know what the future holds. His meaning is, "If I'm to suffer, if I'm to die—regardless of what's ahead for me—I'll look forward to that 'out resurrection' of the dead, for nothing can rob me of that. That's the goal toward which I am pressing."

It is one thing to believe in the coming of Christ at the Rapture; it is another thing to love His appearing as did Paul.

Dr. Bill Anderson was for years pastor of the First Presbyterian Church of Dallas, Texas. A fundamentalist association came to Dallas and rented that auditorium for their conference. Dr. Anderson did not attend any of the meetings. One day Dr. George Gill, one of the most gracious men I ever met, sauntered into his office. Dr. Anderson said, "Sit down, Dr. Gill, I'm very busy here, but as soon as I finish signing these letters I'll talk with you."

So while he was signing letters, Dr. Gill, in his gracious manner, asked, "Have you been to any of the meetings?"

"No, what's your theme?"

"It is the coming of Christ." There was an awkward pause, then he said to Dr. Anderson, "Bill, do you believe in the coming of Christ?"

"Well, I think it's in our confession of faith. Sure I believe it."

Dr. Gill got up and said, "I won't disturb you further. But the difference between you and me is you *believe* in the coming of Christ; I *love* His appearing." And he walked out.

That irritated Dr. Bill Anderson. He thought, *The idea of him telling me I believe it and he loves His appearing!* But he began to think about it, and decided he was right. So he called up his Sunday School superintendent and asked him, "Have you attended any of these meetings?"

"No."

"Well, don't." But I want to ask you to do something. Go home, stay there for twenty-four hours, and look up every passage on Jesus' coming again to see what the Bible really teaches about it. Then we'll have lunch together."

The superintendent agreed to do it. And Dr. Anderson went to his home, got out his Bible and began to check. Twenty-four hours later they met at a certain restaurant. After they had turned in their order, Dr. Bill turned to him and said, "What did you find out?"

"I found out He's coming back."

"I did, too. And I found out something else: I only believed it before; now I love His appearing."

I have heard Dr. Anderson tell this incident many times. And I never have met any other person who so wanted to see Jesus as Dr. Bill Anderson did. He never preached a sermon without mentioning it. Regardless of his subject, somewhere along the line he would say, "He's coming. He's coming back."

The Apostle Paul was looking forward to that 'out resurrection.' The 'out resurrection,' you see, is the Rapture of the Church, because the rest of the dead will not be raised until the end of the Millennium. And the Old Testament saints are not to be raised until the end of the Great Tribulation period. The Apostle John calls it the "first resurrection."

Have you ever stopped to think, friend, what the coming of Christ really means? Most of us think, *Boy, it will get us out of this old world.* Paul says in effect, "I'm not worried about that. It will get me into His presence." That's the important thing. This man has come a long way from being a brilliant young Pharisee. Has he not!

This verse reveals the fact, as does the next verse, that Paul never expected to be made perfect, a complete saint; until then. Paul did not believe that you could become sinless in this life.

12   Not as though I had already attained, either were already perfect; but I follow after, if that I may apprehend that for which also I am apprehended of Christ Jesus.

Perfect here does not mean perfection in the way we think of it. Rather it means perfect in the sense of maturation. Paul is saying, "I have not yet reached that place of full growth. I'm not yet what I'm going to be at the Rapture." The Apostle John puts it like this:

> Beloved, now are we the children of God, and it doth not yet appear what we shall be, but we know that, when he shall appear, we shall be like him; for we shall see him as he is [1 John 3:2].

Paul was looking forward to that day, but he had not yet arrived. You and I meet folk today who think they have arrived. My friend, none of us will arrive in this life. And that's the reason we ought to be out on the racetrack running because we have a long ways to go.

That I may apprehend that for which also I am apprehended of Christ Jesus. Paul means this: "He apprehended me for a purpose, and I want to apprehend that purpose and accomplish that in my life."

13   Brethren, I count not myself to have apprehended; but this one thing I do, forgetting those things which are behind, and reaching forth unto those things which
14   are before, I press toward the mark for the prize of the high calling of God in Christ Jesus.

Brethren I count not myself to have apprehended. In other words, "I have not yet arrived."

This one thing I do. That is, "I have now gotten my life down to where I know there is one thing I am to do." You and I, friend, live in a complex age. It is wonderful to whittle your life down to one point and say, "This one thing I do." Talk about the simple life—if we could get the Christian life down to where we should have it, it would really be an uncomplicated life. Paul says, "I haven't arrived, but I've learned this one thing." What is it?

Forgetting those things which are behind. It is marvelous to be able to forget those things that are behind. Memory is a wonderful thing. But memory plays over the keyboard of the past, and we often let our memories start drifting, taking us back into the past. It is possible for a Christian to spoil his testimony and his service by constantly living in the past. I'm getting to that reminiscing age, and I'm fighting it for all I'm worth. Yet I find myself constantly saying, "Now twenty years ago . . . this is the way we did it." Let's forget the past with all its achievements and mistakes, and not let it be a handicap for the present.

Reaching forth unto those things which are before. Paul says, "I'm on the race course, and I'm on my way to the Rapture." Do we really believe in the coming of Christ? Well, if we do, we're out there running. That's where we find those who believe in His coming.

I press toward the mark for the prize. What is the prize?

The high calling of God in Christ Jesus. We are going into His presence. We are going to be with Him. We are going to be like Him. These are things that Paul says are out yonder in the future for him.

15   **Let us, therefore, as many as be perfect, be thus minded; and if in anything ye be otherwise minded, God shall reveal even this unto you.**

As many as be perfect—now what does he mean by that? I think I can illustrate this by my orange trees. My three orange trees are loaded with fruit this year. Some of the oranges are still green, but for this particular time of year, they are perfect. They are perfect oranges. But if you come and see me in a month, they are not perfect oranges if they stay just like they are now. You see, when Paul says "perfect," he means arriving where one should be in maturation. Another illustration would be that of a baby. Suppose we have a baby here seventeen months old. My, what a wonderful baby he is—wins a blue ribbon. But if you see him seventeen years later and he is still saying, "Da-da," there is something radically wrong. Maturation is the thought Paul had in mind.

Be thus minded—having the mind of Paul, pressing on toward the same goal.

If in anything ye be otherwise minded, God shall reveal even this unto you. Paul believed that God would lead and guide a believer in his life. And this is something else, friend, that is so desperately needed today. We ought to stay very close to the Lord in these days in which we live. He can and He will lead us.

16   **Nevertheless, as to that which we have already attained, let us walk by the same rule, let us mind the same thing.**

17   **Brethren, be followers together of me, and mark them who walk even as ye have us for an example.**

Paul's example, you see, was their standard. That is a tremendous statement to make! I wish we all could say that.

18   **(For many walk, of whom I have told you often, and now tell you even weeping, that they are the enemies of the cross of Christ,**

Now I do not mind saying that there are many men who fit into this category today. They do not preach Christ crucified as being essential for salvation.

19   **Whose end is destruction, whose God is their appetite, and whose glory is in their shame, who mind earthly things.)**

That means they are carnal. They live for self and self only. They are proud of what they should be ashamed of.

PAUL CHANGED HIS HOPE FOR THE FUTURE, *verses 20, 21*

20   **For our citizenship is in heaven, from where also we look for the Savior, the Lord Jesus Christ.**

Citizenship is *conversation* in the Authorized Version. An even better translation is that made by Mrs. Montgomery: "For our city home is in heaven." I like that. But the way I would prefer to translate it is this: "We are a colony of heaven." Let me give you my reason. Picture now the folk to whom Paul is writing. They live in Philippi, which was a colony of Rome. It was one of the few cities in the Roman Empire that was classed as a colony. In these cities lived the Roman officials. People living in Roman colonies dressed like the folk in Rome. If you wanted to get Rome's latest styles, you could go to Philippi because they would be on display there. These cities had the same laws and regulations that Rome had. And the people in Philippi obeyed the laws that were made in Rome. Everybody living in a Roman colony was a Roman citizen. In Philippi they would have been very glad to tell you, "My citizenship is in Rome." Now Paul also was a citizen of Rome, but what he is saying here is "Our citizenship is in heaven." Or, "We are a colony of heaven."

What does that mean? It means that the believer, since he is a citizen of heaven, is to take his orders from up there. He is to obey the laws from heaven. As someone has said, "All the way to heaven is heaven." A believer's life down here should mirror all the way to heaven. That is exactly what Paul is saying. This is the future.

21   **Who shall change our lowly body, that it may be fashioned like his glorious body, according to the working by which he is able even to subdue all things unto himself.**

Lowly body is *vile* body in the Authorized Version. If you think of *vile* as meaning "evil," you are missing Paul's thought. Another has translated it "body of humiliation." I am not satisfied with that, but prefer *earthly* body—"He shall change our earthly body." This body that we have is an earthly body, subject to all kinds of limitations. It is adapted to this earth, which is the reason it is difficult for man to go into space unless he is wearing a space suit or is in a module. He is not naturally equipped to go up there. Our bodies are earthly bodies. Paul is saying that when Christ comes, He will change these earthly bodies with all their limitations, and He will give us a body like His, a glorified body. Or, as Paul puts it in Corinthians: "It is sown a natural body; it is raised a spiritual body . . . (I Corinthians 15:44). The wonder of it is this: You and I will have a body throughout eternity. I don't know what that does for you, but it does a great deal for me. I never liked the notion that in heaven I would have wings, or be just a spirit drifting out into space. I'm very well satisfied with the fact that I'm a man. Although I'd like to have another body—this one is wearing out—I sure want a *body*. Paul says it is "sown" a natural body. That is, this body that we bury is subject to disease, subject to accidents, subject to all the vicissitudes of life down here. And this body is to be changed—sown a natural body and raised a spiritual body.

Years ago in New York City there was a meeting of the theologians of that day. Most of them there were liberal at that time. Dr. Goodspeed read a paper before this assembly. (He was quite a Greek scholar, by the way, but I would not accept his translation of the New Testament because he had a way of substituting adjectives for nouns which weakened the translation. For instance, he translated John 1:1: "In the beginning was the Word, and the Word was with God, and the Word was *divine*.") Well, the paper he read dealt with 1 Corinthians 15:44—"sown a natural body; raised a spiritual body." The point he was trying to make was that the resurrection is just spiritual. That is, the emphasis is on the spiritual, and the resurrection is not to be a bodily resurrection, but a spiritual resurrection. That is all it means. Several of the theologians present made a motion that the paper be published. Then Dr. A. T. Robertson, who was a much greater Greek scholar than Dr. Goodspeed ever was, got up and said, "I want to ask Dr. Goodspeed a question." There was a moment of silence, then Dr. Goodspeed agreed. So Dr. Robertson said, "Dr. Goodspeed, which is stronger, a noun or an adjective?"

Dr. Goodspeed could see the direction he was moving, but he said, "Well, of course, a noun is stronger."

"All right, now let's look at the passage of Scripture you took today: 'It is sown a natural body; it is raised a spiritual body.' *Body* is the noun; *natural* is the adjective. The noun *body* is the only thing carried over in resurrection. The adjectives tell us that the body we have now is a natural *body*; the body we are to get will be a spiritual *body*. It is the *body* that is raised from the dead."

So, friend, you'll never be able to read that paper, because after that the assembly decided not to put it into print after all.

Paul, writing to the Philippians, said, "This body of humiliation—we're to lay it aside, and we are to have a body that will be like Christ's glorious body." From that day on the Damascus Road when Paul met Jesus Christ he began moving toward the time (which is still future), the 'out resurrection' of the dead, the Rapture. ". . . Christ the first fruits; afterward they that are Christ's at his coming" (1 Corinthians 15:23). My friend, what a tremendous challenge this is.

As a Pharisee with religion Paul was willing to go over to Damascus and arrest Christians. But when he met Jesus Christ, and got out on the race course for Him, he went to the ends of the earth to make Christians. What a change had taken place in this man's life!

POWER
FOR CHRISTIAN LIVING

CHAPTER IV

Outline:

1. *Joy—the Source of Power, verses 1-4*
2. *Prayer—the Secret of Power, verses 5-7*
3. *Contemplation of Christ—the Sanctuary of Power, verses 8, 9*
4. *In Christ—the Satisfaction of Power, verses 10-23*

We come now to the last major division in The Epistle to the Philippians: the Power for Christian Living. Actually all the preceding are valueless if there is not *power* for living. In this section the key verse is: "I can do all things through Christ, who strengtheneth me" (verse 13).

God gives here a program for power. A philosophy is no good unless there is power to execute it. The pattern is no good unless you have a dynamic that will enable you to follow it. And certainly you would never be able to win the prize unless there was power. So Paul spends a great deal of time here on the program for power.

JOY—THE SOURCE OF POWER, *verses 1-4*

The word *joy* is not emphasized today. We hear the two words *love* and *peace* more than any other two words in the English language. Why not *joy?* Joy is not mentioned in this current movement at all. Have you noted that these three are the fruit of the Holy Spirit? "But the fruit of the Spirit is love, joy, peace . . ." (Galatians 5:22). Why is it that the world talks about love and peace, but not about joy?

The reason is that joy is the one they cannot imitate. Not only is the word absent, but the experience of joy is absent. We seldom hear about joy until Christmas comes around. Even in our Christmas songs we have stretched a point. I've often wondered what Isaac Watts would do if he heard us sing his "Joy to the World" at Christmastime! If you will read the words thoughtfully you will see that it has nothing to do with the birth of Christ. Isaac Watts wrote that song for the second coming of Christ. My friend, this old earth will never know joy until Christ returns. When "earth receives her King" then it will be "Joy to earth, the Savior reigns!"

Unfortunately, joy seems to be absent even from the lives of many believers today. Because of the absence of joy, we have lost our power. The church has lost its power because of that. The Word of God should be a joy to the believer. Some folk criticize me because I seem to have a good time reading the Bible. It's a wonderful Book and it's just filled with humor, my friend. It's lots more humorous than many books I'm reading today. And it's lots more humorous than our news weeklies. I read them to keep abreast of current events, but to me they are propaganda sheets, and boring. But the Bible is a Book that has joy in it! What myopic viewpoints even Christians have today!

1   **Therefore, my brethren dearly beloved and longed for, my joy and crown, so stand fast in the Lord, my dearly beloved.**

My brethren . . . my joy and crown. You see, it depends on what makes you joyful. What brings joy to your heart? Well, Paul tells us what brought joy to his heart. In substance he said, "When I came to Philippi I suffered a great deal. I was beaten; I spent time in prison. But many of you folk came to know Christ. You are my joy and crown. The fact that you came to the Lord because I brought the Word of God to you, this brings joy to my life here and now—and it will mean a crown when I get into His presence." Now do you have a program that is an improvement on that one? Joy here and a crown over there. This is the thing that Paul had in his life. And you just can't beat that kind of an arrangement.

Dearly beloved and longed for. Notice the tender relationship he had with these believers in the city of Philippi.

Stand fast in the Lord, my dearly beloved. There needs to be stability in the Christian's life.

2   **I beseech Euodia, and beseech Syntyche, that they be of the same mind in the Lord.**

He comes now to the only problem in the Philippian church. He said at the beginning that there was one little ripple on the surface, but it was not serious, and Paul didn't even mention it until near the end of his letter. I have often wondered what the problem could have been. I imagine that probably Mrs. Euodia was president of the missionary society, and Mrs. Syntyche was president of the choir. Each one thought she had the church parlor reserved for Tuesday afternoon. When both groups arrived at the same time, it was rather warm for a few moments. Mrs. Syntyche and Mrs. Euodia had a confrontation. That caused a little ripple in the church, and these two women weren't speaking to each other at this particular time. An old Scotch elder was called upon to read this passage before the congregation one night. His pronunciation was atrocious, but his interpretation was marvelous. He read, "I beseech Odious, and I beseech Soon-Touchy, that they be of the same mind in the Lord." When one that is odious and one that is soon touchy rub together the fur will fly, and we see that occasionally in our churches. Well, we are not told what the background was, only that these two women were not of the same mind.

3   **And I entreat thee also, true yokefellow, help those women who labored with me in the gospel, with Clement also, and with other my fellow workers, whose names are in the book of life.**

Help these women who labored with me in the gospel. In this epistle we learn of the prominence of women in the early church. Now that I am no longer a pastor I can say this (I always said it reluctantly or very carefully before): I believe that the reason women become preachers today or move into areas like that is because women have not been given their proper place in the church. The office of a deaconess, even if it exists in the church, is treated very lightly. I think there ought to be women serving as deaconesses who meet as a board as any other board of the church, and should have the same authority. Women in the early church occupied a very prominent place. Some women feel as though they shouldn't take an office in the church at all. Why not? Some churches would not survive if women were not functioning in the church. When I was a pastor, a missionary came home who had done a wonderful job on the field. When she was to give her report to the church, she asked, "Dr. McGee, should I stand at the pulpit? I don't think I ought to." I said, "Why not? You've got as much right to stand there as I do. You get right up there and give your report." I do not believe in women preachers at all because that is contrary to the teaching of Scripture; I do believe women are to be given the proper place in the church. It is apparent that women did have a very prominent place in the early church. Paul says here that these two women, Euodia and Syntyche, labored with him in the Gospel. That is a pretty good sign they had a prominent place.

4   Rejoice in the Lord always; and again I say, Rejoice.

This is a commandment to a Christian, to a believer. Don't tell me, "Oh, I keep the Ten Commandments." Well, I don't think you do keep them, but the point is what do you do with *Christ's* commandments? One of His commandments is "Rejoice in the Lord always." Do you keep that one? Now don't say, "Well, if I had been in Paul's position, I could have rejoiced." My friend, he was in Rome in prison when he wrote, "Rejoice in the Lord always." Therefore, in any circumstance a believer should have the joy of the Lord in his life.

George Mueller was asked one time, "What is the secret of the joy in your life? You are always a radiant Christian. What is the explanation? Are you that way all the time?" His answer was something like this: "No, a great many mornings when I get up I do not have the joy of the Lord in my life. But I get my Bible, and I read it until I have the joy of the Lord in my life."

Our relationship with God is like a car in that when you neglect something on it, it will give you trouble and you will have to have some work done on it. Many Christians today neglect to have checkups. They don't come in to get their battery recharged. How can a Christian get his battery recharged? From the Word of God. The only charger the Lord's got in the world today is His Word. It is the *Bible* that will bring joy into the life of the believer.

There is power in joy.

You will recall that in Nehemiah's day they had a great Bible reading. After Nehemiah had finished building the walls of Jerusalem, they set up a pulpit at the Water Gate, and there Ezra read in the Scriptures from morning until midday. Many of those people had been in Babylonian captivity and had never in their lives heard the Word of God—never had. And hearing it for the first time overwhelmed them. They began to mourn and to weep. So Nehemiah sent out the word to all of them:

Then he said unto them, Go your way, eat the fat,
and drink the sweet, and send portions unto them for
whom nothing is prepared; for this day is holy unto our
Lord. Neither be ye grieved; for the joy of the LORD is
your strength [Nehemiah 8:10].

n other words, "Your power is in your joy—don't weep!" A great many
people seem to think that God commanded fasting and wearing sackcloth
and ashes. God never did that. You won't find that in the Word of
God. Of the seven feasts that God appointed for His people, every one
of them was to be a time of rejoicing. Over and over they were told
this; "Ye shall rejoice before the LORD your God." I honestly think
that sometimes on Sunday God would say to some folk, "Why don't
you stay home? You've got a sour face; there's no joy in your life at
all. What kind of a testimony are you for Me? I dont want you to
go to church. Stay home and pull down the shades so no one will see
you. You're a disgrace to Me." My friend, we should have joy in our
lives.

Three words: *love, joy, peace.* They talk about love today. They talk
about peace today. They don't talk about joy. The joy is to be found
in the Word of God, friend. It is when you and I come to the Word
of God that we have joy in our lives.

Now there is *power* in joy, and the world outside has learned this.
We seem to have forgotten it. There is a great deal of visitation that
is being carried on today (I've talked to several preachers about this)
and one thing is being left out of the instructions for visitation. This
is it: when you knock on a door and someone comes to the door, radiate
joy in your life. Don't be a sorrowful Christian. Let me illustrate how
the world has taken this over.

The Fuller Brush man calls at our house on Saturdays. He is not
a sorrowful fellow by any means. I don't know whether he is having
trouble at home or not, but he sure radiates joy. One Saturday morning
my wife had gone to the market, and from my study window I saw
him coming. I thought, *I'll ignore him because I'm busy, and I'm not
going to fool with brushes today.* So he came and pushed the doorbell.
I let him push it. He pushed it two or three times. I thought, *He'll
leave now.* But he didn't leave. He knew somebody was in the house,
so he just put his thumb down on the doorbell and held it. Finally
in self-defense I had to go to the door. When I opened the door, I
expected him to be a little irritated because I had made him wait. But

no, he was happy about it. Everything pleased him. He greeted m
joyfully, "Dr. McGee, I didn't expect to see you today!"

"My wife has gone to the market. She'll see you the next time yo
are around." But that wasn't enough for him.

"My, isn't this a wonderful day!"

It was foggy and dreary, but to him it was a wonderful day. I d
not know how he did it, but in the next ten seconds he was in th
living room and I was holding a little brush in my hand. Then I couldn
order him out—he'd given me a little brush. And so I stood there listenin
to his sales pitch. When he had finished I said, "Now look, I don
buy brushes and I don't need one. My wife generally buys from you.

"Oh yes, she does."

"Well, she'll probably buy next time, but I haven't time to look a
them. I'm busy this morning."

So he thanked me and started down the walkway *whistling!* Yo
would have thought I had bought every brush he had! I met a ma
who trains Fuller Brush salesmen, and I told him about this experienc
He said that they were so instructed; they are trained to radiate joy.

As I thought about this, I realized how important it is for a believ
to have the genuine joy of the Lord fill his heart and life as he knock
on doors or as he performs any service for Christ. Joy is the sourc
of power.

Rejoice in the Lord. Our rejoicing is to be *in the Lord.* Where d
you find your fun? In a bottle? In the things of this world? Genuir
joy is found only in the Lord. Every now and then I meet a believ
like that. And I wonder about him. A preacher friend of mine has ha
a great many trials and tribulations, yet he is a most joyful fellow. Or
day I asked him, "Were you always like this?" "No," he said, "not unt
I became a Christian. I used to drink heavily just because I felt s
sorrowful and because I didn't want to face life. It's been wonderf
to be a child of God and to have the joy of the Lord in my life!"

PRAYER—THE SECRET OF POWER, *verses 5-7*

No Christian who is a prayerless Christian can have power in h
life. A prayerless Christian is a powerless Christian.

5   **Let your moderation be known unto all men. The
          Lord is at hand.**

Moderation is a word that is translated many ways. If you will check this word in different translations you will find that no two are alike. It is a word that means many things. The best I have heard is Matthew Arnold's interpretation. He called it "sweet reasonableness." "Let your sweet reasonableness be known unto all men." In other words, be a reasonable person. We should be dogmatic, certainly, but we should also be reasonable. As someone said to a group of theologians, you ought to approach it from the viewpoint that the other man may be right. Sweet reasonableness—let's not be dogmatic about little issues.

The Lord is at hand. This is not a reference to the coming of Christ. Paul is not saying that He is coming soon. Rather he is saying that the Lord is present and He is listening in to your conversation. He is standing very close to you all the time so that whatever you say or do is known to Him. Dr. Chafer used to put it like this, "Secret sin on earth is open scandal in heaven." The psalmist makes it very clear that our sins down here are open before Him. And so Paul is saying that we are to be joyful Christians; we are to be reasonable Christians because the Lord is right here listening in. He is with us all the time, and we ought to be conscious of His presence. We ought to be conscious of Him when we're driving; when we're in our place of business; when we're in our homes. Many believers are losing sight of this today. Yet His presence is one of the most precious things in a Christian's life. To lose it is to lose the reality of Christ. I read a letter that came in today from one of our radio listeners. She wrote, "I've been a church member for years, but now for the first time Jesus Christ is a reality to me." How many folk are like she was. We need to practice the presence of the Lord Jesus Christ in our lives. This is what Paul is talking about.

6   **Be anxious for nothing, but in everything, by prayer and supplication with thanksgiving, let your requests be made known unto God.**

Nothing . . . everything. What Paul is doing here is putting in opposition two indefinite pronouns. And the indefinite pronouns are *nothing* and *everything*. What he is saying here is "Worry about nothing; pray about everything." There are probably no two words in the English language as mutually exclusive as *nothing* and *everything*. Nothing is nothing unless you try to include something. Everything is total inclusion—nothing can be outside. They are antipodes apart.

"Worry about nothing." What does that mean? Does it mean that a child of God is not to recognize existing problems? For instance, are we to act as if sin and disease are not a reality? Certainly Paul never put his mind out of gear; he never adopted a crazy philosophy like that. Then why does he say, "Worry about nothing"? Because we are to pray about everything. That means to take God into every detail of your life. A dowager in Philadelphia, years ago, went up to the late Dr. G. Campbell Morgan and asked, "Dr. Morgan, do you think we ought to pray about the little things in our lives?" Dr. Morgan said to her, "Madam, can you mention anything in your life that is big to God?" It's all little stuff, isn't it? And He wants us to bring all of it to Him. Many of us wait until we get to the crossroads or until a great problem faces us before we pray. But if we had the background of praying about everything, then when we reached the crisis, we'd be able to bridge over it. A great many people pray about *some* things in their lives, but they do not just open their lives to the Lord. In my own life, I used to try to fool the Lord.

For instance, I went through seminary with an old, beat-up jalopy. And when I began my ministry, I had a second-hand car. My officers used to say that I was a disgrace to them driving that old car because it made people think they didn't pay me anything. But I drove that old car until I got interested in a girl. Then I decided I needed a new car. So I went to the Lord, and prayed this way, "Lord, I need a new car for visitation. My officers think I ought to have a new car." Well, sure I'd use it for visitation, but the real reason was I wanted it to court that girl. But I didn't tell Him that. The Lord knew all the time what the real reason was. Why didn't I just come out with it and tell Him? I think He would have been very gracious. He was, finally, and I got the new car. But I should have been open with Him from the start. We ought to make all the details of our lives matters of prayer. Our Heavenly Father *wants* to hear, wants us to bring our petitions to Him. Worry about nothing; pray about everything.

With thanksgiving, let your requests be made known unto God. A commentary I read interpreted this to mean that when God hears and answers our prayer we are to come back and thank him. Now I have read Paul's writing enough to know that if he had meant this, he would have said it. Paul always expresses himself distinctly and clearly. He was a master of the Greek language, which is a very versatile language, and he meant what he said. Paul is saying that when you come to God in prayer, making a petition to Him, you are to thank Him right there and then for answering it. God will hear and answer your prayer.

Somebody says, "Wait a minute. I've got unanswered prayers." I disagree with you. You don't have unanswered prayers as a child of God. It is almost sinful for a Christian to say, "I have unanswered prayers." What a reflection that is on your Heavenly Father! You are saying your Heavenly Father won't listen to you, that He won't hear and answer your prayers. What you really mean is that you didn't get the answer you wanted. If you are a child of God you don't have an unanswered prayer.

Let me illustrate this on the human plane. My dad died when I was fourteen years of age, just the age when a boy thinks his dad is about the greatest. I know now that he drank heavily and had other faults, but he was a good father. And I can say to you today that I never made a request of him that he didn't hear and answer. But most of the time his answer was no. And my dad's no was more positive than his yes. His *no* ended the discussion. But he gave an answer to my every request. And I have lived to learn that the wise reply to most of my requests was no—although I did not think so at the time!

Now I find that my Heavenly Father says no to many of my requests. And it is the best answer He can give. Again let me illustrate.

When I was a young pastor in Texas, just married, I went to St. Louis to candidate in a church. It was considered a strategic, outstanding church. After I'd preached twice that Sunday, I was given a call by the church. Then later they had to come back and tell me that the denomination would not permit them to call me. As I said, it was a strategic church and they needed a church politician there—which I was not, never claimed to be, didn't go into the ministry for that purpose. But I felt that the Lord had let me down. How I whined and complained to Him! I felt that He had made a great mistake by not letting me go to that church as pastor. Several years ago Mrs. McGee and I came through St. Louis and went by that church just to see. It had gone into liberalism. Things have happened there that I'll not mention. I said to her, "Do you remember years ago when I thought I should have had the call for that church?" She said, "Yes," I said, "I thank God that He heard and answered my prayer the *right* way—not the way I prayed it." I can look back on my life and see other times when it would have been almost fatal if He had answered my prayers like I prayed them.

When God says no, it is the best possible answer. But we don't like it that way. Why? Because actually we are praying, not in the Spirit, but in the flesh. When we don't get the answer we ask for, it is evidence that we are out of the will of God. Instead of whining about unanswered prayers, we need to get into the position where He can answer our prayers the way we pray them—that our will may be His will, and His will our will. Paul is saying, "Worry about nothing; pray about everything. And when you go to God with your request, thank Him right then and there because you are going to get an answer from your Heavenly Father." That, my friend, adds reality to prayer. Strauss, years ago, said, "Prayer is a fool talking to himself." Well, it might have been for Strauss, but it's not for God's children. God hears and He answers prayer.

7   **And the peace of God, which passeth all understanding, shall keep your hearts and minds through Christ Jesus.**

We enter this passage of Scripture (verse 6) in anxiety, with worry, and we come out with peace. What has happened? The motto: prayer changes things is not always accurate, nor is that always the purpose of prayer. The storm may still be raging, the waves still rolling high, but we'll have peace. In our anxiety we want God to change everything around us—give us this . . . don't let this happen . . . open up this door—when we should be praying, "Oh, God, change *me*." You can enter in worry, you can come out in peace.

The peace of God, which passeth all understanding—what kind of peace is that? I'll let you in on a secret (this is just between you and me, and I hope you won't let this get out to anyone else). I do not know what that peace is. If I could tell you what that peace is, it wouldn't be this kind of peace because this is the peace that passes understanding.

The Scripture speaks of other kinds of peace which we can understand. There is world peace. We have the assurance that someday peace will cover the earth as the waters cover the sea. It will come through the person of Christ, the Prince of Peace. Also there is the peace that comes when sins are forgiven. ". . . Being justified by faith, we have peace with God through our Lord Jesus Christ" (Romans 5:1). Then there is the peace that is tranquility. The Lord Jesus said, "Peace I leave with you, my peace I give unto you . . ." (John 14:27). That is a marvelous peace, but it is not the peace that passes all understanding. I do not know how to tell you this, but I do know it is a peace in which we don't live at all times. I think it is one of those high pinnacles that God gives us every now and then. We experience it at the height of the storm when we bring our anxiety to Him.

Joy is the source of power; prayer is the secret of power.

CONTEMPLATION OF CHRIST—THE SANCTUARY OF POWER, *verses 8, 9*

A sanctuary is one of the most needed things in our day when so much of what we see and hear is dirty. Hollywood ran out of ideas years ago, which is the reason Hollywood has dried up. Television is boring—same old thing. So what have they done? They have substituted filth for genius. Literature today has moved in the same direction. Christians in this world, where everything that is dirty and filthy is put before us constantly, need a little sanctuary. We need something to think upon that will clean up our minds. We hear so much about ecology today. What about the ecology of man? *We* need cleaning up.

8   **Finally, brethren, whatever things are true, whatever things are honest, whatever things are just, whatever things are pure, whatever things are lovely, whatever things are of good report; if there be any virtue, and if there be any praise, think on these things.**

Finally, brethren—remember that he said, "Finally, my brethren" at the beginning of Chapter 3, when he was just half-way through? Well, now he is nearly through, and is giving his last admonitions.

This has been called the briefest biography of Christ. He is the One who is **true**. He is the way, the truth, and the life. **Whatever things are honest**—He is honest. **Whatever things are just**—He is called the Just One. **Pure**—the only pure individual who ever walked this earth was the Lord Jesus. He asked the question, "Which of you convicteth me of sin?" No one did. He also said, "The prince of this world cometh, and hath nothing in me" (John 14:30). Satan always finds something he can hook onto in me. How about you? But there was nothing in the Lord Jesus. He was "holy, harmless, undefiled, separate from sinners" (Hebrews 7:26). He was **lovely** which means *gracious*. **Virtue** has to do with strength and courage. He was the One of courage, a real man. He took upon Himself our humanity. **If any praise**—He is the One you can praise and worship today.

The thing that is needed today for believers is to get close to Him, a Person. It's not that we come on Sunday and get stamped with a little religion that will take us through the week, and by the time the week is over the stamp has rubbed off and we have to come back to church to get a little more religion. No. Rather, what we need is a constant walk with the Lord Jesus Christ. We are to abide in Him, have constant fellowship with Him. We need more than anything else a sanctuary where you and I can go and have fellowship. I don't mean by this only a sanctuary with a particular geographic location. We can have that fellowship in the office; we can have it while we are driving our car; we can have it when we are in our homes. What we need is constant fellowship with the Lord Jesus Christ. And this is the sanctuary of power. I do not believe that the child of God can have power in his life by having just spurts of fellowship. This is the reason church work today is so futile. The people who are doing it have no power in their lives. The reason is they are not in constant fellowship with Christ. I want to get close enough to Him so I can obey Him, and do the things He wants me to do. That, my friend, is the Christian life. The Christian life is more than following a few little rules and regulations. It is a constant abiding in Christ.

Recently I met with foreign students who came for a convention. A girl from Japan, a very sharp student, made a comment about Americans. She said, "It doesn't seem as if there are many Christians here who are very close to Jesus." I said, "Right. I have to agree with you. They don't seem to be close to Him." This is a thing that is sorely needed today. It would change the lives of Christians in America. Fellowship—the sanctuary of power.

9   Those things which ye have both learned, and received, and heard, and seen in me, do, and the God of peace shall be with you.

A better word for **do** is *practice*. This man Paul could say something that would be audacious if you or I said it. "Practice what I do." Or "*You* do what *I* do." I have prayed for my little grandson this: "Oh, God, don't let him go down the pathway that I went down. Bring him down another way, and to a more wonderful position than I have known." I don't want him to have his grandpa for an example. But Paul could make his life an example to other believers. Tremendous! Paul lived in that sanctuary of power.

IN CHRIST—THE SATISFACTION OF POWER, *verses 10-23*

10   **But I rejoiced in the Lord greatly that now at the last your care of me hath flourished again; of which ye were also mindful, but ye lacked opportunity.**

At the beginning I said that the Epistle to the Philippians is primarily a thank-you note, but before Paul got down to the thank-you part, he dealt with Christian experience. And that's what he has been talking about—just Christian experience. Now he is thanking them for their gift.

But I rejoiced in the Lord greatly that now at the last your care of me hath flourished again. You see, for two years, after Paul was arrested in Jerusalem, they lost sight of him. They didn't know where he was or what had happened to him. When they found out he was in prison in Rome, they took up this offering which they sent by their pastor, Epaphroditus, together with a letter or a verbal message of comfort. Now he is writing to thank them for it.

11   **Not that I speak in respect of want; for I have learned, in whatever state I am, in this to be content.**

How wonderful it is to be content in your present state. Remember that Paul was in prison when he wrote these words. And this is something that many of us should pray about. "Oh, God, make me content with the state I'm in, content with my present position." There are many Christians who are dissatisfied with their lot in life. We get along pretty well as long as life moves smoothly, but when the going gets rough we begin to complain.

12   **I know both how to be abased, and I know how to abound; everywhere and in all things I am instructed both to be full and to be hungry, both to abound and to suffer need.**

In other words, Paul says, "Though I appreciate your sympathy, I know how to live on the lowest plane, economically, and I know how to live on the highest plane. I have done both." Someone has said that it is more difficult to know how to abound than it is to be abased. Well, I'd like to have the opportunity of trying to get used to abounding for a change. But Paul had learned to be content in both states.

I heard Dr. Harry Ironside tell of his experience in this connection. It was his custom to go every year to Grand Rapids for a Bible conference at Mel Trotter's mission. Mel Trotter, you may recall, had been an alcoholic, and after he came to Christ he opened a mission to reach other men who were in his former condition. The owner of a hotel which had just been built in Grand Rapids was an alcoholic, and was led to Christ by Mel Trotter. The man was so grateful to him and so wanted to do something to show his appreciation that he said to Mel Trotter, "When you have a speaker or a visitor come to your mission, you send him over to the hotel. We'll entertain him free of charge. It won't ever cost you a thing." So the next time Dr. Ironside came, Mel Trotter instructed him to go to this hotel where there would be a room reserved for him. When Dr. Ironside arrived at the hotel he was ushered up to the presidential suite. This man was giving him the best the hotel had. Dr. Ironside had never been in a place like that before. It was elaborate. Everything was plush. He went from one room to another, and finally he went to the phone and called Mel Trotter. He said, "Listen, Mel, you don't have to put me up like this. All I want is a room with a comfortable bed and a desk where I can study." Mel Trotter, in that 'whiskey tenor' voice, said, "Listen, Harry, the man who owns that hotel owes me everything. He's provided that for you. It won't cost you anything; it won't cost me anything. You stay there. Paul said he knew how to abound and he knew how to be abased. Now you learn to abound this week, will you?" And Dr. Ironside said, "I sure did learn how to abound that week living in the presidential suite!" Well, Paul knew how to live there too. Also he knew what it was to be abased, by the way.

13   **I can do all things through Christ, who strengtheneth me.**

Through Christ should be *in* Christ. I can do all things in Christ which strengtheneth me.

At the beginning of this study we saw that probably the most important word in the New Testament is the little preposition *in* when it precedes *Christ* or a pronoun that refers to Christ. It is the word that explains what it means to be saved. To be saved is to be in Christ. How do you get in Christ? You receive Him as Savior. You are regenerated by the Spirit of God which makes you a child of God. Paul said to the Galatians, "Ye are all the sons of God by faith in Christ Jesus" (Gal. 3:26). You are regenerated by the Holy Spirit, baptized by the Holy Spirit the moment you believe. What does the baptism mean? It means identification. And that's real baptism, the baptism of the Holy Spirit. (Water baptism is a ritual baptism that gives the visible evidence that you have been put into the body of believers.) "By one Spirit were we all baptized into one body . . ." (1 Corinthians 12:13). The Spirit of God will take a sinner that trusts Christ and put him in the body of believers. He is in Christ.

Now Paul, you see, is in Christ, and he can say, "I can do all things in Christ which strengtheneth me." Now what does that mean? Does it mean that you can go out and jump over your church building? Is that one of the "all" things? Let me use a very absurd illustration to explain what he is talking about.

My favorite mode of travel is by train. I fly because I have to. But the train has lots more romance connected with it, and is much more enjoyable. It gets you there *later*, but it gets you there—which is the important thing. A wonderful train is the Santa Fe Super Chief which runs between Los Angeles and Chicago. That Super Chief can say, "I can do all things a Super Chief is supposed to do in the tracks between Chicago and Los Angeles. I can pull up the Cajon Pass, the highest pass for any railroad in this country, with no problem at all. I can do all things." One night out near Kingman, Arizona, I raised the curtain and looked out—brother, we were moving! Later I was told that we were traveling at 110 miles per hour. The Super Chief can say, "I can go 110 miles per hour, I can do anything in the track between Chicago and Los Angeles that a Super Chief is supposed to do."

Now suppose the Super Chief should say, "For years I have been letting people off at Flagstaff and Williams who talk about going over to see the Grand Canyon. I've never seen the Grand Canyon, and I think I'll go over and take a look." Suppose it leaves the track and starts over to the Grand Canyon. You say to me, "That's absurd." I don't know whether it is or not because one day coming out of Winslow, Arizona, the Super Chief left the track, and it left it on the side toward the Grand Canyon. I have a notion it was headed over there. But it didn't make it because the very minute it got off the track it was a wreck, and as helpless as it could possibly be. You see, the Super Chief can say, "I can do all things *in the track* between Los Angeles and Chicago that a Super Chief should do."

Now, friend, anyone who is in Christ can do all things in Christ. That's my track. That's your track. Not all things, but all things *in Christ*. I can do all things that God has for me to do from the time He saved me to the time He takes me out of this world. *In* Christ I can do all things. That is the satisfaction of power.

There are several things God is very careful with. Have you ever noticed it? One is His glory—He says that He does not share His glory with another. The other is His power. He had tremendous power. But He keeps you and me feeble. He keeps us very weak. He says that He has chosen the "weak things of this world." Why? To demonstrate His power through them. When you and I are in Christ, and we are moving in Christ on those tracks, we are irresistible. There is no stopping us. But the minute you and I step out of that glorious position we have, step out of God's will either by sinning, by our own willfulness, or by lack of fellowship, we are as much a wreck as that Santa Fe Super Chief was, and we are not going anywhere. But if we stay on that track, we can do all things in Christ. "If ye abide in me, and my words abide in you, ye shall ask what ye will, and it shall be done unto you" (John 15:7). We had better make sure where we are before we start asking. It is essential to be in His will.

14   **Notwithstanding, ye have well done, that ye did share with my affliction.**

This is all personal. Paul is expressing his appreciation to them for their present and past generosity.

15   **Now ye Philippians know also that in the beginning of the gospel, when I departed from Macedonia, no church shared with me as concerning giving and re-**
16   **ceiving, but ye only. For even in Thessalonica ye sent**
17   **once and again unto my necessity. Not because I desire a gift; but I desire fruit that may abound to your ac-**
18   **count. But I have all, and abound. I am full, having received of Epaphroditus the things which were sent from you, an odor of a sweet smell, a sacrifice acceptable, well-pleasing to God.**

A Christian in his giving is like a priest of old making an offering to God. When it is made in the right spirit, it is, as Paul is saying to the Philippian believers, more than just making a donation or taking up a collection. It is an offering, an odor of a sweet smell to God. Theirs was an offering that brought glory to God.

19   **But my God shall supply all your need according to his riches in glory by Christ Jesus.**

Thinking of their sacrifice to supply his need, Paul assures them that God would supply all their needs. He doesn't say all their *wants*, he doesn't include luxury items, but all their *needs*.

20   **Now unto God and our Father be glory forever and ever. Amen.**

21   **Greet every saint in Christ Jesus. The brethren who are with me greet you. All the saints greet you, chiefly they that are of Caesar's household.**

Again he refers to the fact that the Gospel had penetrated into the royal family of Rome.

23   **The grace of our Lord Jesus Christ be with you all. Amen.**